HOW TO MARRY THE MAN OF YOUR CHOICE

HOW TO MARRY THE MAN OF YOUR CHOICE

Margaret Kent

WARNER BOOKS

A Warner Communications Company

Copyright © 1984 , 1987 by Margaret Kent
Warner Books, Inc., 666 Fifth Avenue, New York, NY 10103

 A Warner Communications Company

Book Design by Nick Mazzella
Printed in the United States of America

First Printing: July 1987

10 9 8 7 6

Library of Congress Cataloging-in-Publication Data

Kent, Margaret, 1942–
    How to marry the man of your choice.

    1. Dating (Social customs) 2. Mate selection—United
States. 3. Men—United States—Psychology. I. Title.
HQ801.K47 1987   646.7'7   86-40561
ISBN 0-446-51387-3

To my husband,
Robert Feinschreiber,
the man of my choice

Acknowledgments

Books, like marriages, don't just happen. They take planning and effort. Five people were especially helpful in making this book a reality.

Heidi Kent Stollon assisted in the research and preparation of my original marriage course materials.

Bob Feinschreiber, my husband, encouraged me to share these marriage techniques with other women.

Alvaro Zayas ran my office smoothly while I was preparing the book.

Sandy Choron, my agent, was wise in recommending Warner Books.

Bob Miller, senior editor at Warner, devoted a great deal of time and effort to the manuscript.

Contents

PREFACE   xi

INTRODUCTION   1

CHAPTER 1. Learning About Men   13

CHAPTER 2. Dressing for Sexess   19

CHAPTER 3. Meeting Men   35

CHAPTER 4. Dating   53

CHAPTER 5. Selecting the Right Man   63

CHAPTER 6. Helping Him Fall in Love With You   89

CHAPTER 7. Enhancing Your Relationship   101

CHAPTER 8. Praising and Criticizing the
            One You Love   121

CHAPTER 9. Developing Your Sexual Strategy   143

CHAPTER 10. Tying the Knot   161

CONCLUSION   189

Preface

Like most of you, I grew up expecting to have a fantastic husband, wonderful children, a spacious home, and an exciting career. They were supposed to "just happen" as if they were "meant to be." I went to school, attended church, and made friends, but I didn't sit down to plan for my future.

My father, Jack Bradfield, left New Jersey and came to Miami in 1926, back when nobody bothered to count the horses in town. My mother, Hilda Arechavaleta, arrived a decade later from Havana. I was born in Miami during the summer of 1942, the height of World War II. My father was concerned about our safety, and sent my mother and me back to Havana for the duration of the war.

We had a large family in Havana, but an even larger home. My great-uncle was an ambassador from Cuba to many countries. His sons pursued careers in law and medicine, but I was to follow in his footsteps. I expected to have a diplomatic career, a magnificent villa, a phenomenal husband, and lots of children, but it never occurred to me to plan for my future.

In 1948, we returned to Miami from Havana. Learning English wasn't easy, for even in those days Miami had an active Spanish-speaking community. Of course, we visited Cuba frequently.

My life was moving ahead as it was supposed to. As 1958 ended, I was popular with boys in both Miami and Havana, but marriage could wait as I prepared myself for high-school graduation and college in some far distant location to study diplomacy.

Then in 1959 it happened. Castro seized power in Cuba. Just a few months later he announced that he was a communist. Neither property nor people were safe. The time for hopes and dreams was over. I had to go to Cuba to help rescue my family. We evaded the gunfire from Castro's army and eventually made our way to safety.

Our house in Miami was a small one, adequate for my parents and myself. Now we were deluged with uncles, aunts, cousins, and our older relatives. I never knew what sleeping in shifts meant until then. Of course, my plans for European travel and foreign study were long dashed. Many of my relatives spoke no English and were still suffering from the shock and horrors of the Castro takeover. I was needed on the home front, so I enrolled in the least expensive local college I could find, and went to work nearly full time for the telephone company.

Most of my family were engaged in the attempt to recapture Cuba. Only men joined the battle, so I remained in Miami. Robert Kennedy withdrew the U.S. air cover promised by his brother John, and we were defeated at the Bay of Pigs. One of my uncles was captured and tortured, so our personal horror continued.

The Cuban refugees needed a great deal of help to learn English because their departure from their homeland had been so sudden. I organized and taught classes in English through various volunteer programs, but time was limited because of my work and studies. My own personal life was clearly on the back burner.

I was twenty when I finished college and began teaching high school. My social life began again, but I was busy with adult-education programs in the evening. Then, I began graduate studies in Mexico. Soon my graduate degree was completed, and I began thinking about marriage. I now knew that good things don't happen without effort and planning, but I didn't yet have the specific skills I needed to plan for marriage.

In 1967, I was teaching Spanish and French in high school, and English and Spanish in adult-education programs. One of my evening students in the Spanish language program was George Kent. He was originally a Jesuit and engineer, and later became a lawyer and psychiatrist. George had a number of Spanish-speaking patients and clients, and asked me to be his translator.

As an attorney, George had a number of female clients who had been left by their husbands after long marriages and were distressed about their prospects. As a psychiatrist, George had a number of patients who were single women and despondent over their marriage chances. As I worked with George, I realized that there was a pattern to these marriage problems and their solution. By this time, I had fallen in love with George. I decided to turn these patterns into a strategy and use them to catch him.

I put my plan into effect in September 1968. By Christmas, George had made a commitment to me. We were engaged on Valentine's Day in 1969 and married that June.

Many of my friends heard about my success with

George and asked me to help them. I put together a marriage course for six of them, and they each married about six months after the course ended.

Some four hundred people have completed the course since 1969. Every single one of the four hundred were married within four years, and most were married within two.

My first marriage ended tragically. George's unexpected death in 1979 sent me into deep mourning for over a year. Then I decided it was time to start living again and find another great husband—despite the fact that I was almost forty! I also began law school in 1980, completed it in 1983, and became an attorney in Florida.

I met Robert Feinschreiber, a tax expert who has written hundreds of articles and many books, on December 30, 1981. We married December 30, 1984. Didn't I just say it usually takes two years, and here it took me three? Well, I didn't start going out with him for over a year and a half after meeting him.

Of course I used the marriage strategy again with Robert. He is so smart he sensed it. Often he would say, "I know you are doing something different; promise me you won't ever stop."

The course is effective, and a great deal of fun for both the man and the woman. Men will enjoy dates with you more than ever. You'll enjoy your quest, especially your ever-increasing confidence with men as you use the strategies. Don't forget to send me an announcement of your wedding!

HOW
TO MARRY
THE MAN
OF YOUR
CHOICE

Introduction

Look around you, and observe other women. You see women who are not as attractive, youthful, slim, bright, educated, or financially secure as you. But some of these women have men you would want. You may think these women are absolutely undesirable, yet they are successful with men. Why are they married while you're still single?

This book reveals the secrets behind the success these other women have with men. It will show you the techniques you can use in meeting men, developing relationships, and leading the man of your choice into marriage.

You don't *have* to stay single. These strategies will lead you out of the singles jungle and into a happy marriage with the man of your choice. The ten chapters here will show you ten steps to follow to success.

THE PROCESS OF FALLING IN LOVE

This book explores the process by which a man falls in love with a woman. The steps in the love process are analyzed, examined, and categorized. If you are seeking a husband, you need to know how love can be initiated and nurtured.

Love is much more than infatuation. Falling in love, like the development of any other important relationship, is not an endless stream of pleasant experiences. It may surprise you, but the process of falling in love is similar in many ways to the process by which individuals become believers in a religious faith or become patriots to a country. We will examine all aspects of the love process.

You will learn strategies based on the principles of psychology, law, and many other professions. These techniques show you how human behavior can be predicted, molded, influenced, and controlled. The book integrates the behavioral sciences to provide you with advice aimed specifically at leading a desirable man into marriage. If you use these concepts, you should achieve great success with men, and be able to marry the man of your choice.

Use these techniques to facilitate the natural process by which people fall in love. This book is designed for the woman who wants to have a man fall in love with her and marry her, but whose own skills in obtaining the man she wants are inadequate.

If you are worried that the strategies are clinical and there will be no fun in your quest, be assured that just the opposite will take place. You will experience emotional highs from the successes you will achieve.

HOW TO SUCCEED WITH MEN

Doesn't it seem to you that the bitchy women get the men, and that the women who give true unselfish love lose out? If this is the way you view the world of love, you are viewing it accurately, and we will explain why your perception is correct. Bitchy women succeed with men because they make men believe that they are superior women, and that a man is lucky to have them. You will learn how to make a man feel honored that you love him.

EVALUATING MEN

One of the primary causes for marriage failure is that people do not adequately know the individuals they marry. We meet strangers, which is fine, but we often marry strangers, which is an invitation to disaster. These techniques are designed to help you get to know the man as he really is. Better a curtailed dating relationship than a broken marriage. The best surprise in marriage is no surprise.

When a man contemplates marriage to a specific woman, he evaluates her as a prospective wife. Do not be ashamed of evaluating the men you meet as prospective husbands.

You may worry that the evaluation process here will be too conscious and rational, but all too often it is unconscious and irrational, as well as haphazard and incomplete. Sharpen your ability to evaluate men and use your evaluations in selecting the man you want to marry.

Do not invest your emotions with a stranger. You would certainly do some checking before you invested ten thousand dollars with someone you didn't know. Aren't your emotions worth at least as much? If so, investigate before you invest.

Do not waste your emotions on a man until you determine that he is worthy of you. Never become involved with a man because you feel sorry for him or think you can change him.

Don't be a closet heterosexual. If you want to meet

and marry the man of your choice, you've got to go public.

START WITH YOURSELF

Do you want to take charge of your own life, to be all you *can* be? Well, one of the things you *can* be is happily married to the man of your choice.

Your mind is your best asset, for it can improve with use. Everything else eventually sags, wrinkles, or turns gray. The crucial strategies are mental, not physical. Don't make marriage decisions with just one part of your body, whether it's between your legs or behind your ribs. Use your head.

As a starting point, recognize that you are a worthwhile individual. You don't need anyone, whether man or institution, to validate your self-worth. Don't let anyone tell you otherwise.

However, your self-worth is not self-evident. Don't expect the world at large, especially the men in it, to recognize how wonderful you are, at least without a little prompting on your part.

Since you don't need marriage to give you a sense of self-worth, why marry? Because marriage can be fun and enrich your life. You may be a woman who has everything you want—except a husband.

Why So Much Work? Shouldn't You Just "Be Yourself"?

As you are reading this book, you will be asking yourself "Why do I have to expend so much effort? What about the man? Why isn't he pursuing me?" Let's answer these questions now.

In North America alone, there are eight million more marriageable women than marriageable men. If marriage is a priority in your life and you have passed that age where the marriage odds are in your favor, you need updated techniques. The odds were greatly in your favor during your teenage years, but if you are past twenty-five, the odds are increasingly against you. You cannot sit around like a beached whale, waiting for the tides to come in. All you'll get is dead fish and seaweed.

"But shouldn't I just be myself, and act naturally?" Yes, be yourself, but be yourself at your best. You may be wonderful, but even *you* can benefit from self-improvement. You don't need to change your personality, but you might find it advantageous to improve your skills in dealing with men.

What Do You Offer a Man?

Ask a woman what she wants in a man, and she is likely to have specific answers. She may want a tall, handsome, youthful, intelligent, rich, witty, respectful, capable, educated man, of a particular background. Ask the same woman what she can offer him in exchange, and her answer is usually "me."

"Me" is a poor, unspecific answer. The woman must evaluate herself against her competitors. To be successful with her man, she must know what she has to offer and be able to tell the man.

If you are still thinking "I just want to be me!" consider what happens when you go into a restaurant and order a cup of coffee. You don't expect it to be free because "This cup of coffee is for *me*!" You know that "me" is not going to get you a free cup of coffee. Being yourself, and doing nothing more, isn't going to get you anything in life, especially the mate you desire.

A Few Words About Manipulation

This book examines the techniques of manipulation. You will learn how to manipulate others, and how to prevent others from manipulating you without your knowledge. But, you ask, "isn't manipulation bad?"

Manipulation is all around us. We are manipulated by our parents, loved ones, teachers, churches, advertisers, bosses, government, and others. Sometimes we are manipulated for our own good, as is the case, for instance, with wearing seat belts. Even here, there are many facets to the manipulation: The name of seat belts was changed to "safety" belts, laws impose fines for not buckling up, and public-service announcements educate us. The techniques expressed in this book are benign manipulation, like the incentives to use seat belts, or the star your teacher put on your paper to encourage you to keep up the good work.

At numerous points throughout this book, I urge the woman to remain silent, to encourage the man to talk. This is not meekness or coyness, but an important manipulative principle. The person who listens first and speaks second has the advantage because she knows what the first person has said and can respond accordingly. Let others call this manipulation, if they'd like. If the word bothers you, just call it common sense.

TAKE THE INITIATIVE

The man you are seeking can be yours, but only if you take the initiative. Unless you can find diamonds in the street and pearls in your chowder, don't expect the man of your dreams to appear on your doorstep without any effort on your part.

Imagine for a moment that you are considering becoming a gold prospector. Somewhere in the back of your mind you would think about what you would need to carry out your mission. You would think about basic equipment, and of course you would choose a location where there was a probability of finding gold. No matter how ignorant you are of prospecting, you certainly would not expect to find gold nuggets in your front yard, nor would you ever imagine that someone would miraculously ring your doorbell and say, "I understand that you are seeking gold. Here, I've brought you some."

Unfortunately, finding a mate is not unlike panning for gold, yet you may be convinced that there will be some magic moment in your future when you'll meet and marry your ideal prince, all by chance. You may believe that the only requirement on your part is patience, that you should sit back and wait! With this philosophy, all you can look forward to is menopause, and a pet cat for companionship. Wake up! No man is going to knock at your door and ask, "Does a nice girl live here? I'd like to marry her."

These strategies are hot and calculating, not cold and calculating. Love is too important to be left to happenstance. Don't expect magic. You are too mature to believe in Cinderella or Sleeping Beauty. If you want anything else in life, you know you need to work for it, not wait for Santa Claus. The same is true when seeking a husband.

Forget the old myth that you can't find love when you're looking for it. The key is to know where and how to look. Many women have come to believe this myth after getting all dressed up for a social event and meeting no one, and then meeting a man when they're wearing nothing more than jeans and a T-shirt. This does *not* mean that you shouldn't look for love. It simply means that you must learn to look differently. You *can* look for love—and find it.

Why not make your life as pleasurable as possible? Your goal can be to move toward pleasure and away from pain. The amount of pleasure you receive will be your mark of success. If you would enjoy having a husband, do not let anyone deter you from this goal.

USING THE MATERIAL

You are going to attract many men using the marriage strategy. Continue the strategy only on the man you want. This is not meant to turn you into a heartbreaker; it is meant to minimize the risk of someone breaking your heart.

These techniques are powerful. Be sure you want the man before you lead him into marriage. If you apply all the techniques to a man you don't want, you may find that you've painted yourself into a corner!

These strategies are designed for women of all ages (eighteen and older) who can use them consistently. You don't need to be physically perfect to use these methods, but you do need to be psychologically healthy. Of course, make sure the man you select is psychologically healthy too.

Evaluate the methods and strategies, if any, that you now use with men. As you learn our techniques and achieve your marriage potential, you will find yourself changing your behavior with men. Make note of these changes, for they are important for your further development.

For maximum benefits to you, read this book with an open mind. Let us imprint our ideas on you without objections, at least until you have completed your training. If you need proof that the material is valid and effective, do not fight the ideas—test them! But be sure to apply your test correctly. There is usually a large gap between what men do and what they say they do, so be wary of surveys of male attitudes. Go by behavior instead.

You need to recognize when you are succeeding, especially when the man's behavior is fluctuating. You need to know the reasons for praising and criticizing a man. You need courage and guidance to raise your self-esteem and importance to him.

If you review this material often, and you practice what you read, you should become increasingly successful with men. Whenever you achieve some success with a concept, review the material. You may discover a sub-concept that you have overlooked or ignored. Continue to apply these concepts as you reach new heights in your relationships with men. You can develop the zest for winning in your manhunt.

USE YOUR TIME WISELY

Choosing a man for marriage requires considerable effort. To marry well, you need to make good use of your time and your abilities. Since you cannot sift men through giant colanders, you must sift them through your life by learning about them. Then you can pick and choose the best.

It is impractical, impossible, and injurious to your health and wealth to entertain all the men you meet with the traditional routines of food and drink, sex and sweets.

Besides, this is the most unlikely way to find and marry the man of your choice.

Do not ignore the selection process and rush into marriage. An unrestrained pursuit of wedlock may lead to a faster marriage, but after the excitement is over, you may realize that with a little patience you could have made better use of your options. If you are serious about marriage and you apply the techniques of this book in a consistent manner, it should take you less than two years to meet and marry the man of your choice.

YOUR MARRIAGE STRATEGY

The chapters should really be read in order. Chapter 1 teaches you about men and Chapter 2 shows you how to attract them. Chapter 3 tells you how and where you can meet men, and Chapter 4 helps you get more out of dating. Chapter 5 tells you how to interview a man for the job of husband before you audition for the job of wife. Then, if you encourage a man to keep on talking and tell you the events in his life that have emotional meaning, he will talk his way into love with you. Chapter 6 explores the specifics.

You didn't tell all those strange men you met the intimacies of your life, but what do you say to the man you *do* want? Chapter 7 gives you the advice you need to help you enhance your self-esteem and present yourself in a more positive manner.

Praise and criticism are a part of daily life, and essential for the person you are considering as a prospective spouse. Chapter 8 explores these crucial techniques.

Since marriage is a sexual relationship, you need to know how to use sex to your advantage in leading your relationship to marriage. Chapter 9 tells you how. Chapter

10 helps you avoid common mistakes that frighten off men just before the wedding and shows you specific strategies for tying the knot.

DEVELOPING YOUR ACTION PLAN

As you read this book, think of the ways you can apply these strategies in your own personal situation. There is no one quite like you, no one with exactly the same desires, needs, and interests, or the same taste in men. Consequently, you need to know yourself, what you seek in a mate, and what you have to offer. Then, develop your own action plan to personalize the marriage strategy. Happy husband-hunting!

CHAPTER 1

Learning About Men

The more you know about men in general, the easier it will be to learn about individual men. The more you know how men think and how they behave, the more success you will have with the men you meet.

There are three keys to male behavior:

1. The typical man has been influenced predominantly by women during his formative years. As a result, he has predictable reactions to women.

2. A man bases his sexual worth and acceptance as a male on his high-school experiences. He carries that sexual acceptance or rejection to the grave.

3. The male ego is enormous, but eggshell-fragile. Learn about the male ego, for your knowledge of it is one of the best tools for leading the man of your choice into marriage.

WHY MEN ACT THE WAY THEY DO

Males are under the authority and guidance of females from the beginning. From his earliest moments, the young boy is forced into behavior that pleases his mother, female relatives, and female teachers. Each one of these females has a turn at subjecting the boy to her ideas of acceptable behavior, demeanor, and thoughts. He remains dependent on them for his comforts and survival.

Schooling is painful for boys. His female teachers embarrass him with their authority, his subjugation to them, and his mental inferiorities. His female classmates, who mature earlier physically, may also impress him with their superior and faster understanding of the classwork. If the boy rebels, a principal dictates that he be placed under greater control by teachers, who are mostly female.

In school, the young girls are likely to ridicule the boys because of their slower physical development. The girls can do so freely and viciously, since at that age they do not need the boys sexually. This type of intense and prolonged conditioning is hard for the male to overcome, even when he matures.

The male-female relationship begins to change at puberty. Girls begin to experience sexual feelings of curiosity and desire. They start competing with each other for the attention and affection of the more desirable boys. If the young man continues to be dominated by women once he becomes an adult, he is rejected by them because he differs so greatly from their concept of a man. He may be called a sissy, and thought of as unmanly. The male's declaration of emancipation is usually initiated by the older or faster-maturing boys in his class. The male is supposed to surmount years of conditioning and become the aggressor. This process causes the male to develop his large ego, but his ego is fragile because it is self-generated.

USUAL MALE BEHAVIOR

A man has generally been conditioned to the same pattern of conduct or behavior that applies to other men in his society. Not every characteristic applies to every man, but most will apply to most men. Examine these guidelines, and determine the extent to which they apply to the men you know.

1. He believes that he is special or unique.

2. He will marry a woman only if she recognizes that he is special or unique.

3. He wants to be thought as a Casanova, and is polygamous by nature, but he can learn to be mono-gamous.

4. He prefers a good marriage to being single, but does not enjoy the process of getting married.

5. He is very possessive about his mate and will expend considerable effort to keep her.

6. He is conditioned to obey women, starting with his mother.

7. He expects more praise than criticism, but does expect both.

8. He is a small boy at heart.

9. He has a public facade that differs from his natural behavior.

10. He will attempt to follow the mores and customs of the society in which he lives.

11. He is likely to believe in a supernatural being.

12. He is not likely to believe in astrology or fortune-telling.

13. He feels inferior in many ways to other men and will dwell on these feelings of inferiority.

14. He will usually hold himself out as being better than his co-workers or peers, even when he is equal or lower in stature or achievement.

15. He will work to earn a living.

16. He is athletically oriented, and enjoys participating in or watching sports.

17. He is slightly braver than his mate, and will defend her against attacks by others.

18. When ill, he will seek care by a woman who loves him. At an extreme, he will regress to childish helplessness.

19. He enjoys talking about himself.

20. Sooner or later he will want children.

Don't believe that your man is vastly different from other men unless you have clear and convincing evidence to support that conviction. Your man is likely to be as similar to other men, and as distinct from them, as you are similar to yet distinct from other women.

By learning these general features of male behavior, you can better anticipate a man's actions. If a man says something that contradicts these features, such as that he will not marry, it may be wise to disregard his words. If most of the above general statements apply to the man, he is likely to be available for marriage.

CHAPTER 2

Dressing for Sexess

When you go out to meet men, do you go "as is"? Or do you take a shower, fix your hair, put on makeup, and dress in a way you think will enhance your appeal? Are you, in fact, planning your appearance? If so, you are already using your looks to "manipulate" men. This chapter will help you learn how to use this form of manipulation more effectively.

Don't let the power of clothing pass you by, for it can be a major asset in attracting men. If you are afraid to read further because you have limited funds or a body that's not quite fit for fashion, don't worry. As you will see, you don't need thin thighs to marry the man of your choice. The use of clothing to attract men has nothing to do with fashion or size.

Don't feel guilty about using your appearance to manipulate men. You are not going to create a relationship under false pretenses. By being noticed by men, and, most important, by *not* scaring them off, you'll give your new relationships a chance to prosper.

FOR WHOM DO YOU DRESS?

Answer this question honestly. For whom do you really dress? If your answer is "other women," then you are not dressing in a manner that appeals to men. If you dress to impress other women, your clothes are working against you, not for you, in your quest for a mate.

You are dressing to please other women if you buy the expensive fashions of many of the prominent designers. Some designers, but not all, do their best to distort the female form; it's as if they view the female body as unappealing. Women who wear these outfits often appear to men as unfriendly and unavailable for dating. If you wear designer garments, select your designer with a great deal of care. Some fashions can enhance your appearance, but it is hard for most women to know which ones have a positive effect on men.

Chances are, you were first taken shopping by your mother and waited on by a saleswoman. If this is your situation, you probably do not know which clothing appeals to men.

If you dress for other women, these other women may be impressed by the sophistication of the design, the creativity of the designer, or the money you spent. These factors, however, do not impress most men.

If you dress for "business," your business clothes probably emulate men's clothing. The major difference between your suits and a man's suits is that his have pants and yours probably have skirts. If this is your situation, you need a separate social wardrobe.

Many women dress properly for men when they're

not paying attention to their clothing. When these women are not focusing on their clothes, they may wear, for instance, a solid color cotton T-shirt and simple straight skirt. In contrast, when they dress for a date, they look like mannequins wrapped in lace or in unnatural nightwear.

Select your wardrobe carefully, as it can be a real plus in attracting men. Your goal in dressing for a man should be to dress "friendly." Dressing friendly does *not* mean wearing a wet T-shirt or a see-through blouse. Stir his sexual imagination without satisfying his curiosity about your body.

If you want to dress to please men, follow these twenty simple principles.

1. Cleanliness Is Especially Important

If you have the clean, fresh look that a recent shower gives, you can wear a potato sack and still be desirable.

2. Follow the Form of Your Body

What do you think when you see a man in a plaid suit, polka-dot tie, and white socks? You view him as a nerd and reject him. Yet this man may be expending a great deal of effort to meet women, and may dress as he does to gain your attention.

It may surprise you, but women can make the same type of errors in their wardrobe. Women can be nerds, too.

To avoid being a nerd, wear clothing that follows the natural form of your body. Keep the waistline at the waist.

Avoid the waistband under the bosom (the Empire style) or at the hips (the Twenties style). Avoid huge puffy sleeves that make the upper arms appear enormous. Avoid frills, pleats, or gathers that distort your neck, breasts, arms, legs, or thighs. You're better off draping a sheet over your head and tying it at your waist than wearing these uncomplimentary styles.

3. Color

Wear clothing that has a solid color, or at most a small print or stripes that will not detract from the contours of your body.

An outfit that looks busy is like the picture game in which you must find ten things that are wrong. If there are too many distracting items, it will take too much effort to "figure" out your body's shape. Your goal in selecting clothing is enhancement of your appeal. Don't hide your female attributes with confusing patterns.

The basic colors—black, white, red, yellow, and blue—are usually the best. Pink should be avoided unless the style is very sophisticated, because it often connotes that the wearer is a girl, not a woman. Green, orange, and purple are usually less attractive than the basic colors.

4. Fabrics

Consider sex as an electrical force and clothing as the body's insulation. Wear a fabric that "insulates" sexually, but does not create a stiff barrier. Choose a fabric that is soft to the touch and transmits some body warmth. Most natural fabrics—such as silk and soft cottons—and some artificial fabrics—such as silk-like polyesters—are acceptable. Above all, avoid rough, scratchy materials such as metallics, corduroy, or nubby wools.

5. Undergarments

Tight undergarments such as corsets and girdles are a misery of the past. If you own any such instruments of torture, toss them out! No matter how large a woman you are, you are more appealing if your body is unconstricted and natural. If you're bound up in a girdle, you'll look like you're in a body cast or brace. Even if you do look ten pounds thinner, these garments are *not* effective in attracting men.

6. Shirts and Blouses

When you select a blouse, choose one that has an open neckline and small collar. Your blouse should draw attention to your breasts, but not be revealing. Wear a shirt-type blouse or other blouse with buttons in front. These blouses show easy access to your breasts even if the blouse is not the slightest bit revealing. Let the man fantasize even though you don't give him permission to touch.

T-shirts are great. It doesn't take much male imagination to know that in less than five seconds they are off over your head.

7. Skirts

Skirt lengths should be short, but within the normal range for where you live. Skirts that are too short are associated with hookers. If you are sufficiently thin, you can wear a skirt that hugs your sexy body contours. If you are not model thin, though, wear skirts that loosely outline the body and appear easy to raise. Pleats, stiff materials, uneven hemlines, and other devices distort the body to sexlessness. Skirts that button up the front are fine because they stir the imagination.

8. Pants

Men generally prefer to see women in skirts or dresses, not slacks. If you *do* wear slacks, a solid color is best. Avoid plaids and pleats. Jeans are likely to get a positive response because they are snug and outline the body; they also represent casualness and comfort. If you wear slacks other than jeans, wear white or blue or black, not orange or yellow.

9. Shorts

Men like shorts on women. Short shorts are especially appealing, but be sure they are within the norms of your community before you wear them in public. Your shorts should be relatively snug, yet provide you with enough range of movement for your active life. Avoid pleats, even when pleats are in style, as they distort your figure. Select a solid color, not a busy pattern.

10. Bathing Suits

You don't need a bikini—or a bikini figure—to lure men. But if you do decide to wear one, a solid color is usually the best, and be sure the top and bottom match. Make sure your bikini is not the skimpiest, and be sure to stay within the norms of society. And don't go to the other extreme and wear a bathing suit that has a skirt or ruffles.

11. Shoes

Your legs look more attractive if you wear shoes with heels. A slight lift accentuates the calves and creates graceful leg lines. Avoid high heels, though, so that you don't look awkward when you walk or run. Clumsiness isn't sexy. Wear shoes that slip off easily, not shoes with ankle straps.

12. Panty Hose

Garters have been relegated to the category of sexual aides or props; they are no longer items of clothing. When you wear hose, always wear hose that reach high on the thighs. The last thing you want is an elastic stocking band that interrupts a man's imagination as his eyes glide up your leg. Avoid white hose. Natural-color panty hose is preferable, but there are occasions when black net hose may be called for.

13. Hair

Your hair can be an important asset. The style you choose should make a man want to run his fingers through your hair. You don't need beautiful hair—it's "touchability" that attracts most men. You needn't spend much time on your hair. In fact, most women would do better with men if they fussed with it less. Fix your hair for the man's point of view. Cleanliness and softness are the keys.

Ten specific guidelines:

1. Avoid extreme styles—unless you are looking for a man who is an extremist. Stay away from punk.

2. Avoid hair that is too short. Here is a rule of thumb that really is a rule of thumb: Have hair at least as long as your thumb.

3. If you use hair spray, avoid the three *S's*: hair spray that is *s*melly or *s*ticky or makes your hair *s*tiff.

4. Make sure your hair looks soft, not brittle.

5. Once your hair starts to turn gray, the right hair coloring can be a real beauty enhancer. Most men do not like gray hair because it generally makes a woman look older. If you color your hair, be consistent and make sure that roots don't show. Black roots make blonde hair look phony.

6. Don't wear a hat indoors, and don't wear a hat outdoors unless it is absolutely necessary because of the weather. Men love to see a woman's hair.

7. Do not wear curlers in your hair when you are with your man.

8. Avoid frizzy perms.

9. Get rid of those split ends.

10. Get yourself a hairdo that's fun for him to fondle. Keep your hair free of snarls and knots.

14. Jewelry

Are you looking to meet new men, or are you looking to strengthen your present relationship? Your answer to this question should determine the way you wear jewelry, and even the jewelry you wear.

A man looks at your jewelry—or lack of it—as a sign of your availability to him. In particular, he will glance at your hands. If he sees even one ring, he may assume you're not available.

The age-old custom of a man giving an engagement ring and a wedding ring to his woman has a present-day purpose. These rings are designed as barriers to intimidate other men. The single most common mistake widows in search of companionship make is not taking off their wedding rings.

If you are still looking for the man of your choice, avoid rings until you find him. A man views every ring you wear as a commitment ring, given by some other man with whom you have a relationship. You may have bought the ring yourself, or it may have been your grandmother's, but the man you are hoping to meet does not know its origin. Keep your heirlooms in the vault, not on your fingers. When you meet the right man, let him buy you new rings.

A watch is the only jewelry you should wear on your hands or arms (and wear only one watch at a time). Avoid bracelets, as they detract from the man's image of caressing your arms. Also, men generally dislike the noise they make.

There are times when wearing jewelry is appropriate. If you are invited to a gala event where all that glitters is gold, you would feel out of place wearing only your functional watch. For these occasions, the best jewelry is a necklace, especially if it hints at sexuality. A necklace that is tight around your neck may appear unfriendly to the man, as well as uncomfortable for you. Circular necklaces, especially those made of beads, are often a turnoff. Your best bet is to wear a necklace that looks triangular or "plunging," with larger jewels in the center. You will do better wearing one attractive necklace that enhances you than a few different and dissimilar necklaces that distract from your form.

Pendants should be avoided, because they indicate commitment to another man. If you wear a pendant, avoid anything that looks like a locket, or anything shaped like a heart, or a pendant with one single jewel. Also avoid diamond pendants. If you do wear a pendant, wear a pendant with more than one gem.

Avoid wearing visible religious symbols unless you want to attract a man who shares the religious belief that the symbol connotes.

Earrings can be a detriment, especially if they detract from your hair. A man will envision himself nibbling at your ear lobes, and will view earrings that are physically sharp or look like mobiles as barriers. Smaller earrings are preferable to large ones.

There are times at which you should wear no jewelry at all. Do not wear jewelry at the beach, on casual dates, to sporting events, or on the job.

Men look at a woman's jewelry to determine if she is

overly materialistic. If a woman shows too strong an interest in jewelry, and wears jewelry when it is inappropriate, she will turn off most men. Diamonds, therefore, are often not a girl's best friend when it comes to attracting men. Perhaps they are even her worst enemy! Never wear diamonds in a way that could lead a man to think you are committed to someone else. You may be better off with emerald, topaz, amethyst, aquamarine, or other gems.

And one final note: Junk jewelry is just that—junk. Junk is cute on a teeny-bopper, but not on a grown woman. If you wear jewelry, it should be the real thing or nothing at all.

15. Nails

Forget about growing long fingernails. They may impress other women, but they do not appeal to men. Long nails may indicate to many men that the woman is unwilling to do household tasks and is unavailable for recreational activities. Also, men view long fingernails as "claws." Keep your nails clean, at a working length, and without jagged edges.

If you must paint your nails, use clear nail polish or a shade in the red family. Men are more comfortable with painted fingernails on women than they are with painted toenails. If you use nail polish on your toes, limit yourself to clear polish.

You may want long fingernails for gala events, but don't grow your nails just for these occasions. Since you don't want long nails all the time, rely on artificial ones instead.

16. Makeup

One major error that many women make is the excessive and incorrect use of makeup. You are better off with no makeup than with the wrong makeup.

The sexiest part of a woman is her face. If you are looking to attract men, your face needs to look kissable. This does not mean that you are giving a stranger *permission* to kiss you, but you do want him to *think* about kissing you. Unless you select your makeup very carefully, it will hinder rather than enhance your appeal.

Don't surround your eyes with circles of purple. If your eye makeup is obvious to the man, it is excessive.

Men are not eager to rub cheeks with a woman who is caked with powder or foundation. Many men have tasted face powder, and not one has enjoyed it, so minimize its use.

When you wear lipstick, be sure it does not smear. Also: Men prefer to kiss a woman who is wearing lipstick that is in the red family, not some more exotic color.

Careful use of makeup can keep you from looking too young and sexless, or too old and haggard. Older women generally need more makeup than younger women, so your makeup strategy may need to be updated from time to time.

17. Perfume

Excessive use of perfume makes a woman *less* desirable. As with makeup, it is better to use no perfume at all than too much.

If you seek an aroma, choose a cologne or toilet

water rather than a perfume, as it has a more pleasant aftereffect.

And don't expect a man to share your interest in perfumes. He is highly unlikely to know or care about the brand names, but will be offended by a perfume named after an illicit drug.

18. Teeth

You kiss with your lips, of course, but you also kiss with your teeth. Make sure your teeth are appealing.

1. Food particles between the teeth, especially the front teeth, are highly undesirable. Use dental floss if you need it, but not in public.

2. Good dental care is essential, but a man isn't going to be interested in your cavities, caps, and fillings unless he is a dentist. Make sure that your teeth look natural. Avoid looking like a mine waiting to be excavated for gold and silver.

3. If you are missing teeth, get dentures. Missing teeth are a definite turnoff.

19. Overweight?

Are you too fat? Are you worried about your weight? Then here is some good news: A few extra pounds will rarely cost you the relationship. In fact, you are much more likely to lose a man by extreme dieting, especially if the diet involves self-denial. Don't be overly conscious of your weight, or you will make *him* conscious of it.

Do not delay your quest for a mate with the excuse

that you must diet. You don't have to choose between love and food.

However, if you weigh twenty percent more than the standard weight for your height, you will lose a few men. Your losses will climb dramatically if you weigh an extra fifty percent. If your weight is double the standard weight, it will be quite difficult to find anyone to date. Of course, if you are truly obese, weight reduction is in order. If you are under five feet tall and weigh more than three hundred pounds, make weight reduction your priority. More than dating is at stake here.

20. Eyeglasses

Are you wearing glasses to see or to be seen? A carefully chosen pair of glasses will make you more attractive. But how you deal with people also depends upon how well you see them. If your vision is inadequate, you will lose out. No man wants to date someone who fumbles and stumbles.

Contact lenses are not necessary and are not always preferable to glasses. Here are some hints for selecting eyeglasses:

1. Select the thinnest lense that gives you the optical correction you require.

2. Avoid glasses that are too trendy or extreme.

3. A man must be able to make eye contact with you, so avoid reflecting glasses, prism glasses, and other glasses that hide your eyes.

FIRST IMPRESSIONS

First impressions are the strongest and are often irreversible. The first impression you make on a man types you. You don't know what man is waiting around the corner to meet you or is observing you from afar, so act at all times as if you believe in yourself. Do not act like a loser or otherwise allow yourself to exhibit any feelings of inferiority. Present yourself as a winner, and soon you will become one.

CHAPTER 3

Meeting Men

Now that you're approachable, you're ready for the initial step in your manhunt—meeting men. Your ideal mate is scarcer than one in a hundred, and probably closer to one in a thousand, so you need to meet many men to find the man of your choice.

Have a Tourist Attitude

I have a friend who is a travel buff. In her foreign travels, she doesn't hesitate to approach any man for directions, general conversation, or guidance. She can ask a man for an explanation of his customs, his ideals, or his culture. When she is a foreigner in a foreign land, she is not influenced by her culture's illogical controls. She is not selling herself for sex or for marriage, so she feels at ease in her conversations. She treats every man as a book from which she can extract a unique story. This technique works so well that she meets the most desirable and available men, men who seem unapproachable to women in that country.

At home, however, she was tongue-tied. She thought about the ease with which she initiated conversations abroad, and decided that if her tourist personality loosened her tongue, she should be a "tourist" at home. Now she carries a camera and looks "touristy," which gives her the license to approach anyone with any excuse. Men respond quite positively to her initiative.

Saying "Hello"

The first thing you must do is say hello to every man where you live, where you work, where you shop, where you conduct your business, and where you go for recreation. Say hello to every man you are reasonably sure is not a felon.

Many women cannot easily approach a man and say, "You look like an interesting person, and I would enjoy talking to you!" Society has taught them not to approach men they might like. They are pressured to respect social barriers and use "proper" channels to meet men, so they remain in their own social circles, with little chance of meeting new men.

You need some courage to create interest and initiate the contact. Go ahead—you can do it! Most men will respond favorably to your friendliness and start a conversation or give you the chance to begin one. The key is as simple as a smile and the word "hello."

After You Say "Hello"

Your initial hello and conversation with a man should take ten to fifteen minutes. Ask him about himself. If he has recently arrived in your city, for instance, you could use questions such as these:

1. What brought you to this city?

2. What have you enjoyed the most about being here?

3. How different is this city from home?

4. How long do you plan to live here?

5. Has it been easy to make new friends?

6. What interesting places have you found in this city?

7. How are you spending your leisure time?

8. How often do you visit home?

9. How often do friends visit from home?

10. How does this city differ from your expectations of it?

Ask questions that require an explanation rather than a one-word answer. Make it easy for the man to tell you about himself, because in this first conversation he is likely to tell you how unique or different he thinks he is from other men. He will disclose ten to twenty facts about himself in that brief conversation, facts you must try to remember.

Look for any fact or combination of facts that you feel make him different from other men. If you find him interesting, tell him so, and tell him why. Then indicate how he can see you again. Say "I usually have lunch here on Tuesdays and Fridays. Maybe we can talk again next Friday."

If you do not find him interesting, say good-bye. You

need to expand your horizons and meet as many men as you can, but you also need to begin the weeding-out process as soon as possible.

Exchanging Telephone Numbers

When a man asks you for your telephone number, ask him for his as well. Do not give your number to a man who will not give you his. And, to be even more cautious, give him just your office number. Once you have his number, use it. Verify that the number is really his before you date him.

Begin your dating relationship in the daytime and in public places. Delay the more intimate encounters until you are more sure of the man and your relationship with him.

Networking

Networking can greatly increase the number of men you meet and your opportunity to meet the right one.

Keep track of other single women you know, especially those who are not attracted to—and therefore would not be competing for—the men you want. Your female friends can be strong allies in your quest for a mate. Here are some of the benefits you can get from strengthening your female friendships:

1. *Ego-boosting*: Your morale and self-esteem can be damaged by the outside world, but female friends can be very supportive.

2. *Strategies*: You and your friends can discuss specific strategies and techniques. Many of the skills you will learn later in this book, such as interviewing and conditioning, require thought and practice. Your friends can be very helpful.

3. *Information Exchange*: When you meet a man and determine that he is not for you, save his telephone number. Write down some information about him on the back of his card. Now you are prepared to swap numbers with the other women in your network.

You can also benefit from networking with single men who are not prospective mates. They may be willing to introduce you to their friends—and they may be interested in meeting yours.

GETTING THE MAN TO APPROACH YOU

If you want to meet men, you must either be approachable or take the initiative. It is much easier to be approachable. In fact, "approachability" is the primary strategy in meeting men. Many men surround you in your daily life, but you do not even know they exist. Some of these men may be looking at you with great longing, but they are afraid to speak to you because you don't seem approachable.

Some women meet men easily while others do not. Some women go to parties, clubs, and social activities, and don't meet men. Other women can't go to the supermarket without receiving flirtatious looks or being approached by several men. The difference is that one woman is approachable and the other is not.

The Man's Fear of Rejection

Men have little courage when it comes to approaching the women they truly want. A man will much more readily approach a woman he finds slightly attractive than one he is enthralled by; he has less to lose if the former rejects him. That's why those Plain Janes are married and Wonderful You is single and daydreaming.

Men may be courageous on the battlefield and ambitious in business, but they fear female rejection. Yes, they may be avoiding you because they fear you will reject them. A man's sexual image of himself, including his desirability as a male, forms shortly after he reaches puberty, and this self-image rarely changes. Even twenty years later, after years of career success, the man's self-image remains the same, and most men have a very poor one when it comes to approaching women. The man you see as a tall, handsome stranger is a shriveling fourteen-year-old inside, worried about blemishes on his face, his cracking voice, and rejection by you.

In your teenage years, if you were at a school social and no boy asked you to dance, you may have felt overlooked. But think of the boy with a sensitive ego who had to ask the girl to dance with hundreds of people watching. If the girl refused his invitation, he was not just overlooked. He was rejected. The rejection was devastating to him because it felt like public humiliation.

What did that young boy do to avoid the embarrassment of rejection? He approached only those girls who looked friendly and who were happy to return his glances. When it comes to meeting women, men behave as they did when they were boys. Men approach women whom they believe won't reject them.

Friendliness and Approachability

Treat every man as worthy of a friendly hello. This attitude will minimize male fears of rejection. Just smiling a warm hello at every man, whether he is your paper boy or your lawyer, will give you the reputation of being a friendly person and make it easier for men to approach and meet you.

This does not mean that you should offer sexual invitations and longing looks. You can achieve approachability just by smiling and exchanging the civilities of the day and offering one thought of recognition such as "It's always pleasant to see you and say hello."

Do so with every man in your life. You will be developing a habit of making men happy to see you, and you'll become more comfortable with male friendliness. As a result, eligible men will speak to you, including men you thought were unavailable or didn't exist in your world.

Let's imagine that you are at a party and a handsome stranger named Carl catches your eye. You want to dance with him. When Al comes over and asks you for a dance, you say no because you want to keep yourself free for Carl. When Bill comes over, you turn him down for the same reason. Do you honestly think that Carl, who has seen you reject two men, is going to run the risk of being rejected too? Emphatically *no*! But if you had accepted Al's and Bill's invitations, Carl may have mustered the courage to come over.

You may fear that your friendly reputation or your high approachability will attract men, but not the man you want. Don't worry. Your ideal man views himself as superior to other men. For this reason, he is not going to approach you if he is unsure of a friendly reception. After all, he's afraid that if you reject him, people will find out, and it will be a public humiliation. However, if the man of your choice sees that you extend the courtesies of the day to all men, he will dash over.

Preconditions

What if you are especially selective? Suppose you have decided that you want a man who has a certain profession, recreational activity, ethnic background, or religious faith? Recognize that your preconditions will severely limit the number of men you can meet. Since you will undoubtedly be looking for various emotional and physical characteristics as well, your ideal mate may be even *scarcer* than the one in a thousand mentioned earlier.

If you are not dissuaded from these preconditions, then go to places where the men meet your requirements, whether this place is a professional organization, sports center, or ethnic club. However, once you are at that place or event, be friendly to everyone. No matter what group you have selected to begin your quest for a mate, never act like a snob within that group. Smile and say hello to all the men—and the women too.

WHERE TO MEET MEN

No man is going to knock on your door looking to marry you. If you want a man, you must take the initiative. Go where the men are, but find places that do not work against you. Men have images of the types of places they expect their wives to patronize and the types of activities they expect their wives to engage in. By extension, they have similar expectations for their future wives. You may meet men in a variety of places, but some of these places diminish your chances of marriage with the persons you meet there. Here are two common examples:

Bars

A bar is one of the worst places to meet the man you want to marry. He almost certainly isn't there, and even if he is, he doesn't expect to find a wife there. Most men do not view their wives as bar patrons, and these men are much less likely to marry women they meet in bars. There are age differences; older men are more likely to have a negative image of bars. There are ethnic differences, too; the Irish, Germans, and English have a far more positive attitude toward bars than do Italians, Latins, and Jews. The type of bar also makes a difference. Thus, meeting in a sophisticated singles bar in midtown Manhattan may be acceptable, while meeting in a local bar in Brooklyn or the Bronx is not. There are regional differences, and differences based on education and social class. Whatever the case, though, bars are rarely a suitable place to meet because many people act falsely in them, and inebriation changes behavior still further. If you insist on meeting men in bars, meet them after work, not later in the evening. Otherwise, you might spend many hours with someone who won't even remember you the next day.

Churches

A church can be a suitable meeting ground, but only if you are very religious and you insist on marrying someone of the same faith. Otherwise, churches and other places of worship are suitable meeting places only if they are completely open to the public and are nonsectarian.

Twenty Places

Bars and churches are some of the most common meeting places. Since they aren't the best places to find your future husband, where should you look? Some places on this list may surprise you:

1. YOUR JOB. Start with the men at work, but don't stop there. Meet men through your job, as well as on your job, including suppliers and customers. The key to meeting men is having access to them and taking the initiative.

2. BOOKSTORES. It's so much easier to discover a man's interests if you meet him at a bookstore. Also, you are likely to meet a better class of men. Don't be too quiet and shy—a bookstore is not a library. Ask him what books he recommends. Besides, men who are looking for interesting women know to look in bookstores.

3. SUPERMARKETS. Shop in the early evening, when most men are shopping. Ask for help if you can't reach an item on the top shelf, but never act clumsy. Better yet, give *him* the chance to ask for *your* assistance.

4. LAUNDROMATS. Evenings and weekends are the best. Bring extra bleach and fabric softener—you'd be surprised what men forget when they do the laundry! Bring soft drinks too, since laundromats are steamy and rarely air-conditioned. If you see an interesting-looking man, ask him for change of a dollar to use the machines, then offer a soda after you receive the change.

5. LIBRARIES. If there isn't a convenient bookstore nearby, try the library. In a large library, you can pick your section—and men—very carefully. The biggest advantage a library has compared with a bookstore is the opportunity to sit down and meet men at a more leisurely pace. Try the magazine section—it's the least formal, and the most conducive to conversation.

6. BOWLING ALLEYS. Bowling has many advantages over other sports: It's year-round, all-weather, and inexpensive. Besides, it's easier to socialize at a bowling alley than at most other athletic facilities; players are seated right next to strangers, and skill levels are completely mixed. The result: It's easy to meet someone new.

7. AIRPORT WAITING ROOMS. You don't need first-class tickets or even coach to meet male air travelers. If your budget permits, join an airline club and use your membership even when you are not traveling. Men are less afraid to talk to a "fellow traveler."

8. TRAVEL. Be a tourist and meet men wherever you go. Try places that get few tourists, as you will get more attention. And, if you travel in a group, you will meet even more men.

9. DOCTORS' WAITING ROOMS. When you go to the doctor's office or the hospital, you may be able to meet men in the waiting room. But forget this technique if you are going to an obstetrician or gynecologist.

10. CIVIC OR POLITICAL GROUPS. Civic associations and political parties can involve major commitments of time and effort, but they do give you the chance to meet many

interesting men. (However, after a while you may be seeing the same people again and again.)

11. SCHOOL. School is a good opportunity for meeting men, even if you are past usual school age. Almost every school has a contingent of older students, and don't forget male faculty members!

12. PARTIES. It's hard for a party to be active but relatively quiet at the same time, but that's the best type for meeting men. Avoid the loud music and limit the alcohol and you're off to a good start.

13. ACTIVITY CLUBS. Put your activity or hobby to use in meeting men. If you collect stamps or coins, or comic books or records, you can meet men who share your interests.

14. NIGHT SCHOOL ENRICHMENT CLASSES. Evening classes are a great opportunity to meet men. Teach a class rather than take one if you can. Select topics that interest you and also appeal to men.

15. BOATING GROUPS. Boating groups such as the Power Squadron (a national nonprofit boating organization run under the auspices of the U.S. Coast Guard or Navy) usually have far more male than female members. If you like boating, you have a great opportunity for meeting men.

16. SHOPPING. Go to shops that have a lot of men, including places that sell electronic equipment, sporting goods, or tools. But stay out of the men's underwear section.

17. CHARITIES. You can meet kind and generous men if

you invite them to join you in helping charities. Help make sure benefit performances run smoothly, or participate in other fund-raising activities.

18. PUBLIC EVENTS. Go where the action is—the mayor's swearing-in ceremony, a political debate, or a public hearing about a controversial issue. Be an active participant whenever you can, and ask questions.

19. RESTAURANTS. Yes, you *can* meet men in restaurants. This is not necessarily expensive, because the restaurants need not be fancy. Besides, you have to eat anyway. Ask a stranger what he thinks about a particular item on the menu.

20. COUNTRY CLUBS. A costly opportunity to meet a rather limited number of men. Before you join, figure the cost per man. But if you already use the club for other purposes, use it for meeting men, too.

Go Solo

Many women go manhunting with a female friend. This strategy is often a mistake, because a man generally does not approach a woman unless she is alone. You may prefer the companionship of a female friend to going to places alone, but being with another woman diminishes your chances that a man will talk to you. A man may be too shy to approach two women together, even if he is very interested in meeting you. A man will usually approach a plain woman who is alone before he will approach a lovely woman who is with a female friend. If you are with a female friend and a man does approach you,

you also run the risk of his developing an interest in your friend instead of you. If you do go manhunting with another woman, separate once you arrive at your destination.

LOVE AT WORK

We've said that your job is one of the twenty best places to meet men. Men, however, do not usually pursue the women they meet this way. Instead, they typically view their co-workers, colleagues, and other female business contacts as off-limits when it comes to dating and mating. Why are they missing some good opportunities to meet truly desirable women? Let's look at the personal and business reasons.

Personal Reasons—The Fear of Rejection

Because men fear female rejection, they need privacy when they ask a woman for a date. A man must have assurance that if the woman rejects him, the rejection will not become public knowledge. If a woman gossips to her friends about a man she rejected, and men hear this gossip, they will be afraid to try, and she has lost these other potential dates.

Men often feel that they do not truly have access to women they meet in a work context. They don't feel free to come over and ask her out. This problem is most severe when the woman works in a different department or is employed by a separate company. Suppose he is visiting the woman where she works and someone comes over to him and says, "What are you doing over here in the widgits department?" He will be too embarrassed to answer, not because he is ashamed of the woman, but because he fears that rejection by her would become company gossip.

If a man is reluctant to contact you at work, he may try to call you at home. If he can't find your number or it's unlisted, you'll never know of his interest in you.

The problem is worse if you are an executive. Many men would like to meet you, and some might want to marry you, but how many of them could get through your secretary? Because men are often awkward in approaching women they truly want, and they are easily intimidated, your efficient secretary may have weeded out their calls. Or did she take them herself?

A man may try to minimize his potential ego-bruising by using a business meeting as an excuse to see you. Then, if you reject him, he won't take the rejection quite so personally. Perhaps he called you to say that there are a few additional details on the contract he would like to work out with you. You remember him, don't you, the fellow you told to "check it with the legal department"? Or perhaps he told you he wanted your idea about a new product, but you were too busy to give him the time of day. Be on the lookout for male co-workers who interact with you more often than they really have a business excuse for. They may be interested in *you!*

Business Reasons—The Corporate Chaperone

Businesses exert enormous pressures that make it even harder for men to approach women through the workplace. These are four problems that men face:

1. An extension of the incest taboo—that dating a female co-worker is like dating his sister.

2. Company rules against fraternization and nepotism.

3. The laws against sexual harassment: The man fears that his pursuit may be against the law.

4. The general attitude that a man who has time for "woman-chasing" at work isn't doing his job.

Thus, the corporation, in its role of "big brother," has become the corporate chaperone, keeping people apart. What is a woman to do? Can you find love at work? Don't expect men to be up-front about their desires. They are intimidated by women and afraid of the corporate chaperone. Watch them maneuver and manipulate so that they can spend time with women who interest them. You can meet a man on the job or through your job, but the man faces too many obstacles in taking the initiative. *You* have to take the initiative and meet him.

Selecting an Occupation

You usually do not need to change careers to meet more and better men, but you may find it worthwhile to change employers or to change job functions where you now work.

Three traditionally female occupations facilitate marriage. The airline hostess, the waitress, and the nurse succeed with men because they portray approachability, friendliness, and concern with the man's comfort. Men view this effort and attention as an indication that they are liked, and these women therefore have access to men in all social strata.

You don't need a traditional occupation to meet and marry the man of your choice. In fact, you may do far better in meeting men if your occupation is nontraditional.

These are ten occupations you may never have considered that can increase your chances of meeting eligible men:

1. INVESTMENT ADVISOR. You won't meet large numbers of men as an investment advisor, but the men you meet will be among the most successful. You can get to know them readily when they seek investment advice because they will reveal their goals and dreams as well as their finances.

2. MEN'S SHOES SALES. Men usually don't buy clothing from women, but shoes are an exception. Since every man must buy his own shoes, you can meet large numbers of men by selling them shoes. Then, when you meet a man, ask him about his shoes to open up a conversation about his lifestyle.

3. IRS AGENT. You will have access to any man, even the most difficult to meet. Equally important, you will have his attention when you meet him. If you're shy and looking for a man who is very private, this may be the occupation for you.

4. AUTOMOBILE SALES. Most men enjoy buying a car. If you are a knowledgeable saleswoman, you can add to the fun they'll have trying out and selecting a car. You'll be meeting on a positive note because these men will share their enthusiasm with you.

5. BOAT REPAIR AND SERVICE. If you enjoy boating, why not meet men with a similar interest? If you can repair and service a boat, you will be sought after as a crew member.

6. MEDICAL EQUIPMENT SALES. You'll have access to the medical community that the laywoman doesn't. You'll meet large numbers of doctors and technicians, and you can impress them with your knowledge instead of standing in awe of them.

7. SPORTS UNIFORM DESIGN. You'll be meeting many men, most of whom are in excellent physical shape. Besides, you'll start out with physical closeness.

8. POLITICIAN. You'll meet many of the most interesting men in the community. Since you can work on legislation on a variety of topics, you'll have easy access to almost everyone.

9. SECURITY GUARD. You'll have power, and access to many men. You can stop whomever you want and ask him questions!

10. BANK OFFICER. If you're watching over a man's money or helping him borrow in a financial crisis, he'll feel friendly and grateful. Your job also gives you access to much information about him that other women can merely ponder.

CHAPTER 4

Dating

Once you begin meeting a wide variety of men, you will have many more dating opportunities, but if you are looking to marry, your dates should be more than just diversions. Dating is your opportunity to evaluate the men you meet and develop relationships. Do not use your dates to be entertained.

Don't spend your early dates at movies, the theater, or sporting events; these diversions make it harder for you to get to know the man. Your initial dates with a man should give you time for conversation, whether you are going out for coffee, having lunch at a family restaurant, or enjoying a summertime picnic lunch in the park.

Create the opportunity for a man to spend time with you at little or no cost. At first he will invest his money or his emotions, but not both, and you want his emotions. Let him have a great time talking freely about himself. The man will seek you out again just to spend time with you.

PLANNING YOUR DATES

Your dates will be more successful if you plan a variety of activities. These activities need not be exotic, since any change from a man's daily routine provides new sensory inputs. Examine the newspaper for events, and be courageous enough to suggest what to do and where to go. (Be sure that the man has the proper clothing or equipment to participate in the activity, however. You wouldn't want him to go bowling in his three-piece suit!)

Whether you live in a large city or in a tourist town, you can easily achieve variety in your dating activity. Many attractions—boat rides, helicopter rides, sporting events, places of historical interest—will interest you and the man. Even if you live in a small town, you can make your dates sufficiently exciting for him. A moonlight picnic, a test drive of a sports car, bicycle riding, fishing, sunbathing, photography, and walking barefoot in the park can be done almost any place at the right time of the year.

Here is a list of ten interesting things you can do on a date:

1. Visit the oldest building in town.

2. Go to an ethnic restaurant where the food is new to you and him.

3. See your city from its tallest buildings.

4. Take a guided tour of your own city.

5. Visit a newspaper office to see its operations.

6. Attend a lecture on a subject that interests the two of you.

7. Go to a TV station and become part of a live audience.

8. Go bargain-hunting at a flea market, antique shop, or garage sale.

9. Visit a manufacturing plant that offers a tour.

10. Go to a railroad museum, old train station, or automobile museum.

Provide a variety of activities to give him new experiences. Even if the man is reluctant at first to do something different, he will eventually find it very enjoyable. Use your dates to give him sensory inputs. Your strategy is likely to be successful, because other women rarely plan dates effectively. Moreover, you will be getting the man accustomed to spending his dating time with you. Even if another woman temporarily entices the man away from you, he will miss the variety you provided. After his initial curiosity about his new companion is satisfied, he should return to you with enthusiasm.

Vie for every moment of the man's dating time. If the man is not with you, he is out of your influence; letters or telephone calls are not sufficient. The effort you expend on a man could go up in smoke if he spends a week away from you or, worse yet, with another woman.

DATING MANNERS

A man is always judging you on your manners, whether you realize it or not. He may not be conscious that he is noticing them, but he does remember and evaluates the way you act toward him and others.

Old-Fashioned Manners

If the man is elderly, his attitude toward manners may have been formed by Emily Post. He may believe that the man lets the woman (whoops—*lady*) enter the room first, that the man walks on the outside on a street, that the man stands up when a lady enters a room, that the lady curtsies rather than shakes hands, and so forth.

If the man believes in chivalry, and you want this man in marriage, you should let him know that you expect him to be chivalrous and that you expect to be ladylike. You may have to learn pompous formalities, but the sacrifice may be worthwhile for the right man. Be careful, however, that he doesn't treat you as too much of a lady and not enough of a woman. You don't want to be considered a mannequin.

Remember the hats that men wore during the 1930s, 1940s, and 1950s? If the man still wears such a hat, he is likely to have old-fashioned manners.

Modern Manners

Good manners are important to the modern man, just as they were to his parents, but the manners that a present-day man considers to be good manners can be quite different. He should treat you with kindness and expect the same from you, but modern manners are much less sex-differentiated than those in the past.

Here are thirty guides to successful dating:

Telephone Manners

1. Call him. The days of a woman not calling a man
are long gone.

2. Call him at convenient hours. Try not to disturb
him at the office.

3. Keep him on the line only if the conversation is
not dragging. Have something interesting to say or make
the call short and sweet. Let him talk if he wants to talk.

4. If someone calls you while your man is with you,
ask the caller to call back. If your relationship is serious,
let him know who is on the line by mentioning the
caller's name.

5. Whenever he calls you, greet him warmly by
name and always let him know that you're happy to hear
from him.

6. If you are at his home, don't answer his phone
unless he suggests that you do so.

With His Parents

1. Address his parents as Mr. and Mrs. until they
invite you to use less formal names. Don't use familiar
expressions such as "Pops" when speaking to his father!

2. His parents are *always* on his side no matter what
they might say or do, so *never* complain about their son
to them.

3. Chances are that his parents are much older than
you. Don't expect to be waited on hand and foot when
visiting with them. Offer your assistance, but don't in-
trude on their territory if they refuse.

4. Do not assume that his parents have the same values that you have. Avoid comments that might upset them.

5. His parents may want to discuss their interests and tell their stories. Be a good listener.

6. Keep your shoes on unless they remove theirs.

7. Don't wander around their house without permission.

Dating Courtesies and Economics

1. Be considerate of the man's finances when he takes you out, just as you would with a female friend or relative. If he forgets his wallet, offer to pay expenses or lend him money for the date.

2. At a restaurant, when he is paying, order the least expensive item that you like.

3. Invite him to restaurants as your guest, or cook for him frequently.

4. Never act helpless. Even if he finds this behavior cute when you first meet, and most men don't, he'll later hold it against you when it comes to marriage.

5. If you are with your man and you meet someone you know, introduce him proudly.

6. Avoid ethnic slurs, political and religious comments, and even ethnic jokes until you know the man's background, and his attitude toward these remarks.

7. Avoid vulgar language in most situations, especially if he hasn't used the word first.

At His Home

1. Respect his privacy and leave drawers, cabinets, and closets shut until you are invited to open them.

2. When you use his kitchen or bathroom, straighten up after yourself.

3. If you are hungry while at his home, don't raid his refrigerator without his permission, but expect him to offer his hospitality.

4. Tidy up his home just a bit. This will suggest that you would care about creating a nice home environment.

At Your Home

1. Tell him that he is welcome to make himself at home. In particular, invite him to raid your refrigerator any time he wants.

2. When you cook for him, make sure you prepare what he likes! Don't try to impress him with gourmet dishes if he likes plain food.

3. When your relationship is exclusive, give him free access to your home by giving him a key.

4. Share your goods freely. Let him use your phone, stereo, TV, and other equipment.

5. Designate special places for him—his place at the table, a certain chair, his own drawer, and so on.

6. If he wants to help you with household jobs, let him. The more effort he puts into your "nest," the more emotion he is investing in you.

WHAT TO WEAR

Once you have established a dating relationship with a man, you expect him to dress in a manner that pleases you. Do the same for him. Chances are, you will eventually be selecting his clothes, so let him help select yours. You have some outfits that appeal to him and some that don't. Wear what pleases him when you are together.

Dress as a couple. Your clothing and his should match, not clash, whenever possible. Don't wear dots when he is wearing stripes. Better yet, follow the same color scheme, especially when you dress casually. You have more clothing options than he does, so you need to be more flexible.

Appearance continues to be important after a relationship is established, but many women neglect their appearance once they are dating a man on a regular basis. Continue to show him that he is important to you.

COOKING FOR HIM

Virtually all men believe that a woman should know how to cook, and many even expect the woman to cook for them before marriage. Unfortunately, some modern women are lacking in kitchen skills and are likely to lose a man because of this deficiency. Gourmet cooking is not required for most men, but women would do much better in attracting a man if they devoted a fraction of the time they spent in learning bedroom techniques to learning techniques for the kitchen. If you spend a night with a man, whether in your home or his, be prepared to make breakfast for him the next morning. As a rule of thumb, if you do not think enough of a man to make breakfast for him, you should not have spent the night with him in the first place.

Even if you're not used to cooking, you need to learn a few easy recipes that make your meals look fancy and delicious. Some gourmet meals are actually quite easy to prepare. Besides, cooking for a man is an easy way to entertain him, particularly if you have a limited budget.

If you know what he likes, cook it. If he likes to cook, let him cook, even if he leaves a mess. Don't spend more time than a half hour in the kitchen if it means he is alone. Make eating together a special event for the two of you. And if he enjoys the kitchen, try cooking something together—that can be the most fun of all!

PLANNING FOR YOUR NEXT DATE

If you want to see the man again, don't forget to plan for your next date before this date ends. Otherwise, good night may mean good-bye.

CHAPTER 5

Selecting the Right Man

Once you have started dating a particular man, how do you determine if he is a potential husband for you? How do you know if he is that special one man in a hundred—or in a thousand—who is your ideal mate? How do you find out what you need to know about him? How do you know he will fall in love with you? "Interview" him for the job of husband before you "audition" for the role of wife.

The interview should be worked into your casual conversations with a man. Begin the interview as soon as possible during the dating relationship. Do not turn your dates into inquisitions, but use the time wisely to discover what he is really like. Interviewing on dates will lead to a great deal of fun for both of you. There won't be the usual lulls in your conversation, and you won't have the pressure of thinking of some brilliant and impressive thing to say. It can help you feel more relaxed, and he will have a ball sharing his thoughts with you.

You must know the man before you can really love him. A lasting love is based on knowledge, not assumptions and wishes. If to know him is to love him, your love will be real.

YOUR BENEFITS FROM THE INTERVIEW

Your scarcest resource is time. If you follow conventional dating patterns, and focus on entertainment such as movies, theater, and parties rather than on the men you date, you would need many lifetimes to find the man who is right for you. Don't kiss the frogs to find your prince. Since it is no fun to kiss a frog, as well as a waste of your time and risky to your health, a better strategy is to let men tell you about themselves. Cut through the morass by interviewing the men you meet in such a way that they reveal themselves to you, so you can eliminate the unsuitable ones quickly. Then when you have selected the man of your choice, encourage him to continue to talk. Let him *talk* his way into love with you (a technique we'll discuss in the next chapter).

Once you become skillful in conducting these interviews, the man may not realize he is being interviewed, but even if he does, he will still tell you about himself. Men love talking about themselves. You will be sought out by many men if they think you're a good listener.

The interview techniques described in this chapter are designed to enable you to discover a man's virtues and his faults. A man will be eager to tell you about his virtues and reluctant to tell you about his faults, but with a little nudging, you'll know both. Then, when you have made your tentative selection, continue open listening to gain the information you need to praise and criticize him effectively, to win his love, gain his respect, and demonstrate to him that you are the right mate for him.

WHAT YOU'LL LEARN ABOUT HIM

The interview process will teach you a great deal about the man. You will come to understand his self-image, his personality traits, his acceptance by others, his threshold for praise and criticism, and the pride he takes in his achievements. This information is absolutely essential; you must understand where he is coming from so that you can lead him where you want to go.

Discover his self-image as a male in terms of his desirability to females. His self-image may not have changed greatly since his teenage years. If he was rejected or unpopular with girls in high school, he probably lacks the confidence to approach or assert himself with women he finds attractive.

Discover his personality traits, including his attitudes toward the world and toward women. From listening to his early experiences, ascertain his attitudes toward sex, money, religion, family life, and his profession. Also, examine areas in which he feels he must excell to compensate for inferiorities he once felt or for things he once lacked. Look for his threshold for criticism—how much criticism brings on fight and how much more brings on flight, how much praise he needs to feel good about himself, but also how much praise he accepts before he disbelieves its source.

Listen to his stories carefully to determine how he is viewed by others. You will discover his reputation and determine whether it is deserved. This is a beginning-point for the information you should know: What people does he like or dislike, and why? How does he want to be viewed by the world?

A man is proud of his achievements. He wants to tell

someone about his struggles and triumphs, and even his less dramatic accomplishments. If you want to succeed with a man, you need to become his confidante and share his joys and sorrows.

SCREENING

There are three "screening" phases of the interview process, each of which is absolutely essential:

1. Determine if there is something special about the man. Is he worth more than a ten-minute conversation? If not, eliminate him right away.

2. Determine if his values and goals are compatible with yours. Could you live with him over a long period of time? If not, stop wasting your time, however much you may want to believe otherwise about him.

3. Determine if the way he relates to people is compatible with your expectations and requirements. Does he meet your emotional needs?

Let's take a closer look at the three screening phases of the interview process.

Discovering His Uniqueness

The first step in the interview process is to determine if there is something special, different, unique, or exciting about the man. This process is your initial screening of potential mates. Most men are sufficiently interesting to merit your further attention beyond this initial screening.

How do you recognize the qualities that make him special, and even unique? The key is to ask him about himself, instead of telling him about you. You'll have plenty of time to tell him about you later—after you've decided that he's worth it. If you've dated him for several months, and you've had over thirty hours of conversation, you can start your stories. However, it is wisest to keep him talking about himself first, at least until he starts repeating himself.

Values and Goals

Ascertain the man's values and goals early in the dating relationship to determine if he is a potential mate for you. But before you use the selection criterion presented below, discover your own values and goals by answering these questions yourself. Take the time to write down your answers so that you can compare them with his. This comparison demonstrates crucial aspects of your compatibility with each other. Your responses to these questions need not be identical to his, but they do need to be compatible. If he wants two children and you want four, it will probably be a compromisable difference. But it will not work out between you if one of you does not want children and the other does. Look for full compatibility on any issue that is crucial to you, and look for general compatibility on the noncrucial items. Insist on full compatability if the value or goal is a "zenith"—a value or goal that absolutely cannot be compromised.

Here are some questions that you can ask him to help elicit information concerning his values and goals:

1. Do you believe in heaven and hell?

2. Do you believe you will come back to earth in the future as another being? If so, what do you expect to be?

3. How often would you like to go on vacation?

4. What holidays do you celebrate and with whom?

5. Do you prefer living in the city or country? Why?

6. Would you like to visit a foreign country? Which one?

7. Would you ever give up your citizenship? Under what circumstances?

8. What are your attitudes concerning abortion?

9. What would your dream house be like?

10. Under what circumstances would you declare bankruptcy?

11. What is your attitude toward minorities?

12. What are your attitudes concerning capital punishment?

Interpersonal Relations

Ask the man questions that pertain to the way he treats other people and the way he is treated by them. He will probably treat you in a similar manner and expect comparable treatment from you. Then determine if his "interpersonal relations," the ways in which he interacts with people, are compatible with your expectations. This information will also provide you with the basic facts you'll need to lead him into marriage. These are just some of the questions you can ask to elicit information about how he treats and is treated by others:

1. Do you believe that you've enjoyed life more than your friends?

2. When in your life were you most popular?

3. How did you meet your best friend?

4. Do you generally trust your co-workers?

5. Have you or would you ever run for an elected office? Did you win?

6. What's the most money you ever borrowed from anyone? The most you ever lent?

7. When in your life did you feel most alone? Most supported?

8. How many children would you like to have? Why?

9. What makes you angry? What about women makes you angry?

10. What events of your life were more fun in retrospect than at the actual moments you experienced them?

THE LISTENING PROFESSIONS

The interview skills you can use to select some men and eliminate others draw upon the listening patterns of four professions:

1. Law

2. Journalism

3. The clergy

4. Psychiatry

People who succeed in these professions have mastered the skills necessary to become professional listeners. If you want to increase your success and status with the opposite sex, you need to master these skills and use them to your advantage.

Let's take a closer look at the listening skills required for the first two professions (we'll look at the latter two in the next chapter).

Law

Lawyers elicit facts from their own clients and examine witnesses in depositions and at trial. Thus, one of the most important legal skills is getting witnesses to testify. The lawyer controls the witness by asking questions and urging that the questions be answered. Then the lawyer asks related questions to determine if the answers are consistent. You, too, should ask related questions and cross-examine the man, when necessary, to check his answers for consistency.

Journalism

The investigative reporter asks thoughtful but probing questions to elicit information. Each answer usually leads to another question. Reporters want the whole story in a logical sequence, and they don't stop until they get it. Make sure that when a man tells a story, you get the *whole* story.

BASIC INTERVIEWING RULES

The key to good communication is not talking, but listening. We are often willing to talk, but we are rarely willing to listen. You have heard the expression that "talk is cheap." Well, the opposite side of the coin is that "listening is expensive."

The interview process utilizes probing questions, active listening, and analysis of the man's responses. Catalog and process the information so you can use it later. These listening strategies have nothing to do with meekness, for you are not a passive listener. Instead, these techniques will change you from a casual listener to a professional one.

Interviewing is more difficult than it appears, but the skills can be acquired. These are the five basic rules for conducting an interview.

1. Direct the conversation to key topic areas.

2. Let him talk.

3. Show interest and remember what he says.

4. Do not censor his comments.

5. Do not criticize or ridicule him during the interview.

Let's look at these five basic rules.

Conversational Direction

Direct the man's conversation to your interest areas. Discover what he is truly like as a person by asking him about his attitudes, values, and experiences. If you are afraid that you may seem too nosy bringing up a subject out of the blue, say that you read an article in a newspaper, had a dream, were asked your thoughts on the matter, or heard the issue raised on a talk show. Discuss such sensitive issues as abortion, premarital contracts, whose career has priority, and investment decisions.

Let Him Talk

Listen to his stories instead of reciting yours now. Avoid interrupting him, and, in fact, encourage him to fill in the details.

Show Interest and Remember What He Says

Show him with body language that you want to hear about him. Look at him attentively during the conversations; don't putter around. Maintain eye contact and look interested. Encourage him to talk by listening carefully. Focus the conversation on him. When there's a lull, ask him about another facet of his life.

Remember what he tells you about himself. The knowledge you gather will be your key to deciding whether he is a prospective mate for you, and will help you develop your personal strategy.

Avoid Censorship

Do not "censor" his conversation by refusing to listen to a particular topic. (Though later in the chapter we'll examine some exceptions to the no-censorship rule.)

Avoid Critcism and Ridicule

Do not criticize him during the interview phase of the relationship. If you criticize a man for exposing his thoughts, feelings, or experiences, he will become anxious and clam up, or tailor his remarks to avoid offending you. Avoid expressing your own opinions, ideas, and attitudes at this time, so that you can discover him as he really is.

BUT WHAT ABOUT ME?

If you are impressed by a man during your early dates, you may want to tell him your innermost thoughts. Wait. Do not reveal too much about yourself yet. Here are five reasons why:

1. Don't waste effort talking about yourself until you decide the man is a suitable mate for you. There will be plenty of time to talk about yourself and express your ideas later—*if* he passes the interview and the relationship continues. Weed out at least nine out of ten men you meet and then tell your private thoughts only to the few who remain.

2. You may frighten the man away before he knows you well enough. Save some topics, including your hopes and your dreams, until he has invested emotions in you.

3. If you wait until you complete the interview of the man you want, you will then know his needs and will be better able to emphasize attributes that are most important to him.

4. If you tell him about yourself too soon, you may inadvertently censor him or cause him to tailor his description of himself and his values and goals.

5. If you let him do the talking early in the relationship, he is more likely to fall in love with you. Your premature disclosures may interrupt his conversation and stop him from transferring affection to you.

Be prepared to convince the man that you are the right woman for him, but don't make these statements too early in the relationship. If you decide that you want a man for marriage, you will prepare a "sales pitch," one that is personally tailored for him. (More about this in Chapter 10.)

THE LISTENING PROCESS

The listening process is both open and active. Both of these facets are essential if we are to realize our objectives.

It is "open" because you should let the man complete his train of thought as long as he is on a roll. As you listen to the man tell about himself, you will not be totally silent. Encourage him to continue talking by making such comments as "That's interesting, tell me more" or "I enjoy hearing about you." If necessary, prod him gently by making a comment such as "Cat's got your tongue?"

The listening process is active rather than passive because you should evaluate, categorize, and remember what you hear. Then, use this material to elicit and cross-check further information. Pay close attention to what the man is saying.

As a listener, you need to be empathetic. "Empathetic" does not mean "sympathetic." To be empathetic, you show him that you understand his feelings. Don't show sympathy—that you feel sorry for him—unless he is relating an event that has sadness for him.

Also, as a listener, you should be *dis*interested, but not *un*interested; in other words, you should be objective where possible, but you should not be bored. If you are bored, move on, as he is not the right person for you.

HOW TO ASK QUESTIONS

You will be far more successful in eliciting information if you know how to ask questions and you know what questions to ask. Your questions to him should often begin with the word "why."

For maximum benefit, ask questions in the most neutral language that you can, so that the man does not know your views. If he does know what your attitudes are, he may pretend to have the same views in order to win your favor. You lose control of the relationship if you disclose your views too soon.

Ask questions in a specific context. You can use newspapers, magazines, television programs, or books to provide the context: There are always plenty of current events involving politics, religion, sex, money, and other things that matter. Consider these sources as props, and use them to elicit his attitudes. The stories you hear are filled with indications of who the man thinks he is, who he wants to be, how others see him, and who he really is. Discover him as a public person, as a private person, and as a potential mate.

As you listen to a man tell you about his values and his interpersonal relations, you can form a true picture of his personality. Carefully gather information about his behavior with others, because he is likely to behave in the same way with you. Picture what life with him would be like. Focus on money, sex, zeniths, energy, and what he wants in a mate.

MONEY

A person's attitude toward money is one of the more crucial components in marriage, because money touches all aspects of life. If you and your spouse do not share similar attitudes about money, you face a turbulent marriage.

Listen carefully to what the man says when it comes to earning, spending, saving, and financial responsibilities. He is likely to expect you to handle *your* money in the same manner. For a successful relationship, you both should have the same basic ideas about money. Concentrate on the following five areas to learn about a man's financial attitudes.

Survival Anxiety

What amount of money does he require to feel financially comfortable? Some men are happy with a steady job paying $20,000 or less a year. Others need more than $1 million in the bank before they lose "survival anxiety," the feeling that one is vulnerable to economic disaster.

Spending Versus Saving

You should determine what sacrifices the man will make to keep his money. These are some of the questions you should be able to answer:

1. Would he prefer to live in a posh palace or in a simple home and bank the dollar difference?

2. Does he wear ordinary and unstylish clothes rather than purchase new items?

3. Does he pass up favorite foods because they are too expensive?

4. Does he drive an old car because newer cars cost money?

5. Does he refuse to buy anything until it has a bargain price?

6. Is he unwilling to spend a little more just for aesthetics or just to save time?

7. Does the price motivate everything he buys from the cheapest self-service gas to the wine he drinks?

8. Does he go to a movie only at the early-bird price?

9. Does he prefer being cold in winter to paying higher heating bills?

10. Does he insist on sending his children to public schools rather than private ones because public schools are free?

11. Is he resentful of paying for items such as the barber, lawn mowing, or maid service?

If the man resents paying for his luxuries, he will also resent paying for yours. He may even resent your paying for these things yourself.

Or maybe the situation is the opposite. Perhaps you are frugal and you resent a man who spends money for show or for comfort, especially if the funds are yours or they're joint funds. Determine if you and he have compatible attitudes.

Spending Priorities

Ask the man what he would do if he suddenly inherited $100,000. Don't accept a flip answer; ask him to give some serious thought to what he says. His answer will indicate his financial priorities.

Would he purchase a snappy wardrobe? Would he quit work for several years and play, or attend school, or work on a pet project? Would he invest or save all or part of the money? Would he purchase gifts for people who are close to him? Would he set up his own business? Would he give any of it to charity? Or would he treat the amount as too small to bother with?

Family Versus Money

Will your potential mate prefer to spend time with the family rather than earn more money? What are his plans for career and children? Will he work fourteen hours a day, travel a great deal, and leave you to raise the kids primarily by yourself? Does he prefer that you work or care for the children in their tender years— or both? Does he plan to work until he falls apart or take a premature early retirement? Learn his time allotment between earning money and being with his family.

Real Survival

Discover what your man's behavior would be if hard times hit. Gather this information through his discussions about himself. He will tell you how he behaved in the past when money was scarce. Expect the same attitudes if hard times return. If his family was poor or provided him with little money during his teens, chances are he will always have a "survival" mentality and will be very conservative with his money. If, on the other hand, his parents were well-off and he learned to take money for granted, he may spend more wildly as a result.

SEX DRIVE

Sex is another crucial aspect of marriage. Sex is a need. If the man's sex drive is higher than yours, he is likely to do other things for you to secure the privilege of rolling over in bed and finding convenient sex. On the other hand, if your sex drive is greater, you will have to make sacrifices to obtain the sex you need.

Ideally, the two of you should have equal sexual needs, but no two people are perfectly matched. The person with the lesser need for sex usually becomes the boss because the other person must relinquish power for sex. The person with the higher sex drive may try to have a pleasing personality in hopes of getting sexual favors.

ZENITHS AND AVERSIONS

Zeniths are more than goals. They are the goals that cannot be ignored or even compromised successfully.

Sometimes a woman knows all of her zeniths because she has thought about them carefully. Often, she knows some of her zeniths only at an subconscious level. Before you proceed, you ought to know your own zeniths.

If your zeniths and his are in conflict, move on and find someone else. If you interfere with a man's pursuit of his zeniths, or if he agrees to ignore his zeniths, your marriage may be doomed from the start. Do not abandon your zeniths either.

If you have compatible attitudes toward money and sex, and share zeniths, the probability of marital success is very high.

You also need to discover his aversions, those things that he dislikes intensely. The two of you do not need the same aversions, but you must be certain that your aversions are not inconsistent and do not conflict with the other person's zeniths. Zeniths and aversions you should have in common include such things as money, careers, lifestyles, prestige, and fame.

Position, Power, and Prestige

A man often wants to equal and preferably surpass the other men and women in his family in position, power, and prestige.

If his father is a chairman of the board, the son is likely to view himself as a future chairman of the board. His family may have a tradition that he plans to continue of being lawyers, pilots, military officers, politicians, doctors, accountants, musicians, forest rangers, police officers, actors, or undertakers. He may not be able to marry you if you cost him his family dignity by objecting to his occupation.

You are fortunate if you have access to a man's family, because then you can observe for yourself how he reacts to his family's values and traditions. If your man was raised in an orphanage or foster home or suffered youthful deprivations, he may need an exalted position in life to feel important. Be aware of his attitudes toward position, power, and prestige and determine if his attitudes are compatible with yours.

Religion

Religion is a zenith for some men. If a man believes that he was born to be saved, and that life in the hereafter is what life here is all about, he is not going to stay married to a nonbeliever, unless he feels it is his duty to "save" her. If you are a nonbeliever and he gives up saving you, you're out of the marriage. If a man had a religious upbringing, even if he now has no formal religion, he may still have these religious values and expect certain types of behavior from his wife. Know what he expects before you marry him.

Physical Attributes

Most men have an idea of what they want in a woman physically, just as you are likely to know what you want in a man. However, some men have inflexible physical standards. When you interview him, try to discover if his rigid requirements have caused him to break up with women in the past. If you are far from his ideal, his displeasure will eventually surface. Before too long he is likely to go elsewhere to find what he misses in you.

Education

Many men want an educated woman. This is particularly true if his family values education. If you do not have a formal education comparable to that of his female relatives, prepare yourself for further schooling or serious home studies, or realize that you and he may have conflicting zeniths.

Lifestyle

Determine what facets of his life he won't change. Evaluate his preferences for foods, entertainment, hobbies, choice of friends, political views, pets, personal hygiene, and dress style, and try to find out which of these preferences are intractable.

ENERGY

Energy levels between spouses should be similar. Otherwise, the more energetic person may eventually consider the other person to be a dud, and the person with less energy may come to consider the first person to be hyperactive. This energy is a force that relates to physical activities other than sex, from dishwashing to football.

Different energy levels create problems when only one person wants to party, swim, jog, or take long drives. He or she may require little rest or sleep, and may need to be active constantly. The high-energy person usually expects his or her mate to join in the activities. If the mate refuses because of lack of stamina, the other mate may interpret the refusal as a personal rejection. If this pattern of behavior continues over a long period of time, it will likely create serious marital problems, including feelings of frustration, anger, alienation, and rejection.

Observe your potential mate's energy level and decide if you can reach his energy level and if he can reach yours. If your energy levels don't match, plan alternatives where the person with more energy will be content to displace the excess energy. The energetic person can join an exercise spa, bowling team, or sailing club, or have projects around the house that require energy.

WHAT DOES HE WANT IN A MATE?

A man marries for several reasons, especially for good companionship, good sex, and to secure a suitable mother for his children. However, what makes a woman "good" and "suitable" is a value judgment formed differently by every man. When you are interested in a particular man, extract from him the criteria he is using to judge and select his future mate. Good companionship, as far as he is concerned, may consist of a fellow jogger, gourmet cook, an avid camper, or a professional colleague. Find out what's on his mind.

It may surprise you that what a man says he wants in a wife and what he really wants are often not the same. When you recognize his real desires, the things he actually responds to, you can treat him accordingly.

THE INTERVIEWING CHRONOLOGY

Past-Future-Present

To discover what made a man who he is today, ask him first about his past, then about his plans and expectations for the future, and finally about the present. People are usually reluctant to talk about their present attitudes and actions because they fear the information could be used against them. But they will discuss their past and future more readily because that information has less impact on their present lives. For example, at the early stage of your relationship, he will undoubtedly be willing to tell you how much he earned in his first job and what he plans to earn ten years from now, but he might find it highly inappropriate for you to ask him what he earns now.

Start the interview by asking your man to tell you about his childhood. As he continues, encourage him as far as you can. If you are an effective interviewer, you have a little boy before you, reliving the little boy that he was.

Then ask the man about his youth, particularly his high-school days. Use gentle, probing, and pleasant questions. Ask him when he first owned a car, when he started dating, who were his female friends and who were his male friends, what attracted him to particular girls, what sports he enjoyed, and what he liked best and least about school, work, and home life.

Allow the man to communicate whatever he likes. Wait patiently and quietly until he begins to tell you all.

As your man is recalling events of the past, portions of this reminiscence will not be as interesting to you as they are to him because he is emoting as if the events are happening now instead of just being remembered. However, the longer he continues reliving the past, the closer your relationship will become. Encourage him to tell you more. Let him know you share his joys and sorrows.

The more a man talks to you about his past, the more likely it is he will speak about his future. Ask him about changes in his life, what caused them, whether his priorities shifted (and if so, why or when), the goals he has reached, and his new goals. Ask him where he wants to be and what he wants to do at some time in the future.

Be sure to raise—not avoid—controversial topics. As a youngster, you may have been told not to discuss sex, politics, religion, or money. That rule makes sense, if at all, only when you are dealing with casual acquaintances. These four topics—sex, politics, money, and religion—are among the most crucial when you are interviewing men to choose your future husband. Ask questions about anything and everything that is important to you. Then listen to and evaluate his answers.

How Well Do You Know Him?

After you have spent some time interviewing the man, test yourself to determine how accurate and complete your knowledge is about him. Can you predict what his behavior would be under most circumstances? Set up imaginary situations and ask him for his reactions. See if your guesses are correct. Do you know his zeniths? You are going to have to make most important decisions about your relationship with him based on the knowledge you have gained from interviewing him. Make your determinations carefully and accurately.

CONVERSATIONS TO AVOID

There are four types of conversations that should be avoided because they only waste your time and his: hearsay, private topics, trivia, and outrageous claims.

Hearsay

A man may tell you stories of other people's lives that have been told to him. These stories have little value for your purposes because they rarely reveal the man's own values and goals and do not tell you about his relationships with others. Try to redirect the conversations back to *his* life. Stories that pertain to others are called "hearsay" by lawyers; this type of testimony is usually barred from use in the courtroom. These stories have as little value to you.

Private Conversations

Avoid conversations that relate to your private life, the life you do not share with your man. If you are a teacher and he is not, do not talk about your students. Don't tell him about your boss's new hairdo, or the gifts your co-worker received at her shower, or the dental problems of your aunt's sister. In general, he will not be interested in conversations about people he doesn't know unless they are public figures.

Trivia and Idle Chatter

Avoid trivia when you can. Consider anything to be trivial if it cannot affect your life or his. It is a bad sign if someone returns too often to trivia; usually it means that he really doesn't have other thoughts to express, he can't reveal himself to you, or he has something to hide. It is always appropriate to ask, "How does this affect your life?" Tactfully turn the conversation back to him so that you can continue the interview.

Outrageous Statements

Censor your man's monologue when he is telling you something so outrageous that you know it isn't true. For example, if he tells you that he has billions of dollars, that he is the son of Queen Victoria, or that he is the true discoverer of penicillin, censor him by saying that you don't believe what he says, but you find him interesting anyway.

The reason you must censor the man in this limited instance is that if he exaggerates his stories to the point where he can't prove them, he will then be too embarrassed to see you again. You certainly don't want that!

But even if what he says is untrue or downright outrageous, it is still valuable information to you. His exaggerations and lies indicate what is important to him and his wishful thinking. These are important clues to what his zeniths are.

CHAPTER 6

Helping Him Fall in Love With You

Once you have interviewed and selected a man, the next step is to help him fall in love with you. Encourage him to relive the events in his life that have emotional meaning and reveal the emotions he felt for others. As he continues to talk and you continue to listen, he will develop further affection for you. Let him talk his way into love with you.

You can gain his love only if you are an empathetic listener. You need to invest your own time and emotions, so do not use this technique unless you are serious about the man.

THE TRANSFERENCE TECHNIQUE

First, let us examine "transference of affection." When we reveal our thoughts, actions, ideas, or personal history to another person, we also transfer to our listener the emotional feelings for the people and things we are describing. This transfer takes place even if these emotions were long dormant within us.

Transference is regularly used by members of the clergy, counselors, psychiatrists, and psychologists to control behavior and secure loyalty. Many teachers, fortune-tellers, fund-raisers, secretaries, salespersons, and other professionals also use this technique successfully. When you use transference, you can change the direction of the man's behavior to secure his loyalty to you.

Let's take a look at two of the ways the transference technique is used in our society.

Religion

The clergy have the skill to elicit confessions from their parishioners. They encourage the believer to tell all because they offer comfort or forgiveness. The parishioner gets emotional relief from unburdening.

The best-known example of transference of feelings is the Roman Catholic confessional. Once inside the confessional, a person exposes inner secrets, desires, and thoughts to an empathetic listener. "Telling all" makes the person feel important, loved, cleansed from guilt—and therefore grateful. Because the listener is usually anonymous, the positive feelings of warmth and gratitude are aimed at the Church and transferred to the Church.

Psychology

The psychiatrist and psychologist use their listening skills to elicit emotional responses. They encourage their patients to talk freely about events in their lives that have emotional content, and they listen with empathy and interest.

Sigmund Freud discovered that his female patients fell hopelessly in love with him when they told him any thoughts that came into their minds and were listened to without criticism. Freud was not a handsome man, but to prevent his female patients from falling in love with him, he sat out of their sight. However, female patients fell hopelessly in love with him anyway, even though they were talking to "themselves" and could not see him. This was a result of the "transference of affection" phenomenon.

APPLYING THE TRANSFERENCE TECHNIQUE

The best shortcut to a man's heart is to capture the love that he has felt for other women. You can gather all the love in the man's heart and have him transfer this affection to you. Every man who has ever loved can be made to love again—to fall in love with you.

You can gain his affection through planned questioning and uncritical listening. The transference technique is not difficult to apply with a little patience and practice.

Basically, the transference technique is like the interview except that you will direct the conversation toward events in your man's life that have emotional content. Explore with him all his feelings and experiences. Ask him to describe his inhibitions, anxiety, guilt, hostility, anger, pleasure, competence, self-esteem, lust, sorrow, love, jealousy, and dependency.

Encourage the man to disclose his secrets, problems, or peculiarities by asking him to tell you about everything that comes into his mind without exception. This is the main method for uncovering unconscious motives.

Create a friendly atmosphere when asking questions

and listening to your man. Listen warmly to what he says. Your open listening makes it easy and comfortable for him to talk. Open and empathetic listening has a strong seductive effect that bonds the speaker to the listener. This transfer of affection produces profound and lasting loyalty and love for you.

Framing Your Questions

Suppose the two of you are watching a television program. You can let the program serve as a backdrop for your questions.

Don't ask: When did you first watch this show?
Unless you ask: *Why* do you like the show?

Don't ask: Who is your favorite character?
Unless you ask: *Why* do you like that person?

Don't just ask: What is your favorite sport?
But ask: *Why* do you like it?

You and Your Competition

Do you know about your man's first affair, his first car, his first job, and everything else that is important to him? If you do not know the answers to these questions, you are failing to gain all of his affections because you do not have the "open ear" that he needs. Your man is, has been, and will be vulnerable to another woman who knows the transfer of affection techniques. If she induces such a monologue from your man, he is likely to transfer his affections from you to her.

Since this transfer of love technique can be used against you by other women, you need to use it regularly to retain your man's love. If your man's affection for you is not deep enough, transference is a true and tested method of gaining and increasing his affections.

A number of women think so much of themselves that they believe that this transfer of love technique cannot be used on their men by other women. They are adamant in saying that their men would not discuss such personal things. They would bet their last dollar that their men would not relate the events of their lives to someone else! But they would lose this bet, because all men are small boys at heart. They love to tell their stories!

Getting Him Away from "Her" to Talk to You

If the man is interested in some other woman, you can entice him into your corner by encouraging him to talk about his present love interest. This may injure your pride, but it will be effective. Many women make the mistake of not asking about the experiences that their man had with other women in the past; their egos won't permit him to talk about them. Many women consider the man's affairs too painful to discuss, and some women feel that if they start this discussion, they in turn may be forced to reveal their own past sexual activities. Avoid these problems by directing the conversation carefully. Moreover, without complete open listening and knowledge about him, your relationship will be in jeopardy, and you will have missed the man's total affection.

Let Him Talk

Let him talk openly, without interruptions. Even if his answers are not in a logical sequence, they are in an emotional sequence that makes sense to him. If he stops and waits for you to give him some comments about yourself, do so, and repeat some minor incident of your life. Always give him back the opportunity for conversation. As he talks, he will expose to you his inner thoughts. If, in the meantime, you keep your past out of the conversation and don't compete for an analysis of yourself, you will be extraordinarily successful.

One reason that a secretary may marry her boss is that she has learned to let the boss do the talking. Consequently, he talks himself into marriage.

If you have not enjoyed open communication with your man, he is likely to be surprised and shy about answering at first. But keep asking him, and keep telling him that you want to know about him because he is so unique and interesting. Chances are great that he will start communicating with you.

Usually it takes a man about a hundred hours to reveal all the emotional tales of his life. Let him invest emotions in you during these hundred hours. You will know you have reached the end of his emotional history when he starts repeating his stories while saying "I've never told this to anyone before."

As you ask questions of your man, you are planning for the future. To become his indispensable mate, you must be his empathetic listener and his confidante.

Touchy Subjects

As a listener, have "big ears." Help the man to tell you the things that will give him emotional relief. Let him confess. He may not be completely frank in the beginning, but don't be concerned, for frankness will come later. When you begin this process, don't encourage your man to discuss subjects that are unpleasant to him or subjects that he views as particularly private. However, it won't be long before he tells all, including the intimacies of his sex life.

You want him to learn the habit of confiding in you. Encourage him to talk to you as if he were talking out loud to himself. Do not be offended at anything he says; let his mind explore all possibilities. If you are shocked too easily, you will appear unsophisticated or mentally weak.

QUESTIONS TO ASK HIM

When you ask him questions, be sure the questions are predominantly positive, but not totally positive. Review the proposed list of fifty questions to see their general positive slant. These are only a few of the questions you can ask; use your imagination and make up your own. Once the man has warmed up by answering some of these questions, and you do not laugh or scold or compete with him and reveal your own attitudes, he'll probably talk your ears off. Great!

1. What was he like as a little boy?

2. What is the first thing that he can remember?

3. Who were his favorite relatives?

4. What games, clubs, hobbies, sports, and other activities did he like or dislike, and why?

5. What parts of his childhood would he like to relive?

6. What does he remember about his first day of school?

7. Did he enjoy school? Why or why not? What was his favorite grade and who were his favorite teachers?

8. What does he remember best about his home life?

9. What does he think is the most important factor in a home life?

10. What does he consider the most important part of growing up?

11. At what age did he first like girls?

12. At what age did his voice change?

13. Did he ever want to be a girl?

14. Did he enjoy having brothers? Sisters? Why?

15. Did he have enough money in his youth? Enough clothing?

16. How did he see himself then? And now?

17. Who was his first date? Where did they go?

18. Who were his other dates or steadies? What did he like and dislike about each one?

19. What jobs did he have?

20. What is the extent of his education and job experiences? What were his emotional reactions to his jobs, his fellow employees, and his bosses? What were his ambitions?

21. What does he think his natural gifts are?

22. What does he consider his strong points? Weak points?

23. What is his medical history? Experience with orthodontics?

24. What is his favorite holiday, music, television program, and pastime?

25. What has he ever built?

26. If he had a million dollars, what would he do with it?

27. If he were to cast himself in a movie, what role would he play?

28. What is his definition of an ideal woman?

29. Does he like pets?

30. What are his thoughts on dress?

31. If he could be anything he wanted to be, what would he choose?

32. Who are the ten most important people in his life?

33. Does he have any hatreds?

34. Who are his friends?

35. What characteristics in people does he respect? Hate?

36. Where would he like to live? What country, state, city, house, apartment?

37. If he could exchange his physical features with others, what would he exchange and with whom?

38. What are his views on aging?

39. How religious was his family?

40. What has been the best year of his life? Why?

41. Who educated him in sex? What were his sexual experiences?

42. What are his views on sex? Who should teach sex and who should indulge in it?

43. What are his political views?

44. Where would he like to be buried? Is he against cremation?

45. If he had to be stranded on an island with only one other person (not yourself), who would he choose? What one book would he choose?

46. What are his prejudices?

47. How would he complete the sentence, "Man is ———?"

48. Is he easily accepted by others?

49. Does he believe in an afterlife?

50. Has he ever fathered a child? Does he want children?

These fifty questions are only a springboard to other questions. Use them to prod your man into talking freely. Do not make the mistake of asking these questions in one sitting or administering them as a school exam. Do not under any circumstances photocopy this list, hand it to him as a questionnaire, and ask him to fill it out. Instead, use the questions to loosen his tongue. Moreover, use them only when he runs out of his own ideas. Only then do you start him off again, and if necessary, on a new subject.

Additional Questions

When you prepare questions for your man, go back to his past, even before high school. Some of these questions depend on his background, or on his answers to prior questions. Here are the sort of follow-up questions you might ask him:

1. When did you first think of becoming a writer?

2. Who was your mentor when you first entered business?

3. What first evoked your interest in science?

4. What additional degree, if any, would you pursue?

5. What are your strongest leadership traits?

Use these questions to get him to open up to you. Let his answers serve as the starting point for other questions you'd like to ask him.

CHAPTER 7

Enhancing Your Relationship

Once you select your future husband and help him fall in love with you, you need to enhance your relationship so that it ultimately attains the fullness and completeness that both of you expect from marriage.

A relationship does not develop on its own. It takes nurturing, even if the two people are in love. You both must expend considerable effort to bond your two lives together and become one.

Even if a relationship begins with physical attraction and culminates in sex, the intermediate steps require conversation. Don't let any gaps in your communication skills destroy the relationship. Talk your way into his heart.

ENHANCING YOUR SELF-WORTH

You will do better with men if you increase your own self-worth, especially if you fear that the man will reject you for any one of these three reasons:

1. Your level of general intelligence.

2. Your lack of knowledge about his career.

3. Your background, culture, or speech patterns.

Do not let any of these deficiencies keep you from the man of your choice. Here are some shortcuts you can use to feel more secure with him.

What You Need to Know

To deal successfully with a man, you must know something about his job or business and his intellectual interests. You may have your own profession, but you must also learn about his. You'll need at least conversational familiarity with law, engineering, economics, carpentry, or any other field that is of interest to him.

Stimulate your own thinking and gain awareness of the world around you by going to a library or bookstore. Select nonfiction books about a variety of subjects, from stocks, exercise, and economics, to dieting, boating, and furniture-building. Examine the book jackets of a large number of these books and then skim some of the more interesting ones. Finally, select a book that you want to read thoroughly. Each step in this process will give you many new ideas to discuss with your man.

Newspapers and magazines can also enhance your general knowledge, as can television and radio. Most men expect their women to be knowledgeable about current events; be sure to watch the news every day, especially if you haven't read the newspaper.

Mental Stimulation

You can dazzle your man by providing him with at least ten new ideas to think about each week. He'll develop a hunger, and then a need, for the mental stimulation these new ideas provide.

A good reference book can provide interesting topics of conversation. Prepare for each date by learning something of interest to the two of you. If necessary, prepare for your date much as a teacher prepares lesson plans for class. If the man values mental stimulation, you will have to do your homework.

If he values formal education, and you are less educated than he is, learn at least one new thing each week that *he doesn't know!* He'll complain about you showing off your learning, but his image of you will change for the better.

Each of us knows something most others don't know. There must be at least one subject of general interest that you can speak about intelligently for an evening when your man takes you to dinner with his boss or with a client.

Your man should be comfortable in knowing what you'll say. Be prepared to talk about some interesting aspect of your work or an outside activity; have at least one twenty-minute speech or anecdote you could deliver if you needed to.

Show enthusiasm over *something;* enthusiasm is contagious. Even if your listener doesn't know much about what delights you, your enthusiasm will incite his. He'll feel alive and vibrant being with you. No man wants the responsibility of entertaining a woman forever. He wants to know that she has her own interests in life and can also do her part in keeping him amused.

Show your intelligence whenever possible. Start by

asking the man questions about his own field of knowledge so that he will answer with ease. Then ask harder questions. His respect for your intelligence will be raised proportionately to the number of intelligent questions you ask. You will start to acquire the "meeting of the minds" necessary for a successful marriage.

Use Your Mind to Attract Men

To increase a man's interest in you, develop some familiarity with those topics that are near and dear to him. These subjects are usually the man's occupation or outside activities. He accepts compliments and praise from any source, but he eventually makes you earn his mental respect. If he does not respect your mind, he will not marry you.

It is of crucial importance that the man believe you have the mental capacity to think clearly and deeply. If he believes that you can think as well as he thinks, then he will believe you can feel as deeply as he does. Remember that he is looking for a woman who he thinks is worthy of him.

The Man and His Job

No man will ever intimidate you mentally if you become knowledgeable about his field and its limitations. Learn the specific purposes and limitations of the man's profession or trade. You can then speak knowledgeably and impress him with your interest. It is especially important to learn the gaps in his knowledge so that if he tries to overwhelm you with the importance of his job, you can diminish it to its appropriate level.

Rarely will a person marry someone who puts him up on a pedestal. Do not be overly impressed by a man's job, no matter what it is. Never allow any man to treat you as inferior just because you lack the knowledge to perform his job. Tell him that the mere knowledge of a specialized trade or profession does not add materially to a man's wisdom. Say things such as "I'm sure there are other adequate people doing similar jobs" or "How many lives did you save today?" or "When do you expect the Nobel Prize for your work?"

Each man overemphasizes the importance of his specialty or trade to gain identity and recognition. He wants you to believe that his occupation requires a lifetime of constant practice, but this usually is far from the case. If the man brags that he is a physician, point out to him that he lacks a law degree and is not qualified to enter the field of forensic medicine. If the man is a lawyer, tell him that he needs a CPA certificate to go with his law degree in order to be a tax expert.

Each occupation has a vocabulary all its own. If you learn a few dozen words he uses in his job, you will be very impressive to him. Read a how-to book that pertains to his occupation. For example, if your man is a carpenter, be able to identify the different types of saws he uses. He will be pleased by your interest.

Eliminating the Medical Mystique

Consider the field of medicine as an example of how to learn and apply the limitations of an occupation. If you want to marry a doctor, you need to know something about the field of medicine, especially its limitations, so that you are not in awe of him.

To appreciate how little is known in medicine, examine a medical dictionary. You will find many terms ending in "itis," which indicates a "condition," and "osis," which means "condition of." These terms are often used when the illness remains a mystery to the field of medicine. *Dermatitis* is just a fancy word for a skin condition, *arthritis* is a swelling of a joint, *sinusitis* is a sinus inflammation, and *halitosis* is just another word for bad breath.

By learning a few Latin and Greek roots and suffixes, you will more readily understand medical vocabulary. Thus, "tomy" means "to cut out," and "mastos" means breast, so a mastectomy is the surgical removal of a breast. "Hyster" is Greek for uterus, so hysterectomy is the removal of the uterus.

Once you master the mystery of medical terms, you are better prepared to date a physician and speak intelligently with him. Use your knowledge to ask about the causes of various diseases ending in "itis" and various conditions ending in "osis." A doctor may use jargon to sound more impressive. What would you think of a physician who tells you "You have a swollen breast and I can't explain exactly why. You may have scratched your nipple or something may be wrong inside." You would be impressed only if he used the medical terms: "You are suffering from mastitis. In my opinion it could be caused by an abrasion of the nipple or a bacterial infection."

If you are interested in a physician, you need to speak his language; your general familiarity with medical terms will help make you more desirable to him. Do the same with any professional.

SPEAKING OF YOU

Now it's time to talk about you. Aren't you glad you didn't tell all those strange men you met the intimate details of your life? You remember them, the ninety or ninety-five percent of the men you met with those early hellos and have since eliminated from further consideration. Now you have reached the stage where you enjoy the men you are with and consider each as a potential mate. As you make the transition between casual dating and a serious relationship, you need to know what to say to these few select men who deserve to hear about *you.*

THE IMPORTANCE OF COMMUNICATION

Once a relationship becomes serious, you both need to speak up and express your thoughts and feelings. If either of you is overly private or withdrawn, the relationship will be in jeopardy. If the man is too quiet, do not assume all is well. Draw him out. Even if you are shy or reserved, you need to tell him about yourself.

Some quiet people take great pride in being self-sufficient, even to the point of hiding their personal needs or wants. These folks display affection by performing their duties in their relationship, but not by talking about the relationship or its problems. Expressive people take pride in verbalizing their wants and needs. Their goal is total communication, and they show affection by talking about whatever is on their minds.

Some people have a very strong sense of personal privacy and consider inquisitive people to be nosy. Yet people who are caring and concerned will inquire about a loved one's private life and expect some answers. When these responses are not forthcoming, the silence is interpreted as a lack of love, trust, or interest in maintaining a relationship.

If you are the emotionally quiet type, an expressive person may view you as withdrawn, arrogant, unfriendly, or cold. If you are expressive, a silent type may view you as aggressive, rude, or overbearing. These differences are a source of misunderstanding. In the following examples, she is taciturn and he is expressive, but in some relationships it's the man who is too quiet.

SHE: He should know that I love him and that I'm unhappy with the rut we are in.
HE: She must be pleased with our relationship or she would speak up.

SHE: He is supposed to know what I'm thinking. He should know my needs and I shouldn't have to ask him. If I'm thirsty, he should bring me a drink without expecting me to ask.
HE: I'm dying of thirst. What good stuff do you have in the refrigerator?

SHE: I'll bite my lip for now. If I can't stand the overall relationship, there's no point in complaining. I'll get out.
HE: If something is bothering me, you're going to hear about it. I can't read your mind, so how can I expect you to read mine?

Taciturn and expressive people are likely to misinterpret each other's intentions. To avoid this sort of misunderstanding, encourage your partner to spend at least fifteen minutes each day telling you what's on his mind, and be sure to express yourself as well.

SPEECH PATTERNS

Do not let poor diction or weak vocabulary impede your relationship. Social-class distinctions are based partially on money and partially on education, but evidenced primarily by speech patterns. If your speech is deficient, the man may view you as a member of a lower social class and reject you for marriage.

You always try to look the best that you can. Try also to sound the best that you can. Choose the best words you know when you express yourself, especially if your man is well educated, but don't use big fancy words when plain ordinary words will do, or you'll sound pompous, pretentious, and phony. Use more precise words when they apply; for example, instead of using the word *smell* as a noun, use *odor, aroma, scent,* or *fragrance* to describe what you mean. Avoid most forms of *get,* such as *get in* or *get to.* Also avoid *yeah, sort of, pretty* (when not describing looks), *you know,* and *kind of.* Examine the following ten words and phrases and then compare levels of speech so that you can raise your own speaking level:

Avoid:	Use:
lower-level words	*higher-level words*
kid	child
nah	no
ain't	isn't, aren't
mad	angry
bother	annoy
false teeth	dentures
glad	pleased
guy	fellow, gentleman
brainy	intelligent
pig-headed	stubborn

Enhance the man's image of you by recalling words you know but have been too lazy to use. If possible, correct his speech by paraphrasing what he says in a superior vocabulary. For example, if he says "I'm mad," you say "You mean you're angry—*dogs* go mad." Every time you improve his conversation, you will increase his respect for your mind.

Your speech will improve if you talk to a man as if your old English teachers were eavesdropping. Or pretend you're a wealthy woman speaking to a friend and her servants can overhear her. A man who listens to you will recognize your careful speech.

Your rate of speech can categorize you as either a thinker or a scatterbrain. A deliberate delivery of words conveys intelligence, while overly rapid speech indicates impulsiveness and can make your words sound insignificant. Avoid incomplete sentences. Think before you speak. Form complete sentences in your mind before speaking.

WHAT SHOULD YOU TALK ABOUT?

The subject matter of your discussions can be divided into three categories:

1. Public topics

2. Private topics

3. Mutual topics

Whenever you discuss a topic, consider whether it is public, private, or mutual. Surprisingly, you should discuss public topics and mutual topics, but avoid private subjects, ones with which only you are familiar. You may see these vividly in your mind, but it is very difficult to describe them to your man in a way that evokes his interest and curiosity. As a result, people who talk about private topics are often boring.

In contrast, public topics are good ones because both of you are likely to be familiar with the subject matter. Years ago, many women were taught to avoid controversial topics such as sex, religion, and politics. But *don't* avoid controversial topics; they create sensory inputs and destroy boredom.

A topic is public if strangers are aware of it and could plausibly participate in the discussion. Events described in your newspaper and happenings you see on television are good examples. Here is a list of ten public topics:

1. The weather

2. An athletic championship

3. Politics

4. Abortion

5. A new clothing style

6. An upcoming election

7. Political unrest in a foreign country

8. A murder or kidnapping

9. Rumors of a new cure for cancer

10. A current movie or concert

Topics are private when they pertain to the individual lives of you or your man, but not to both. These are some examples:

1. When you first meet a man and he does not know your family, discussions about your relatives are private.

2. Unless your man works with you, discussions about your job and your co-workers are private.

3. Unless he is a neighbor, conversations about your neighborhood are private.

4. Discussions about vacations you took before you met him are private unless he has also been to these vacation spots.

5. Discussions about your friends are private unless he knows them too.

Mutual topics pertain both to you and your man. These are some examples:

1. The foods you both enjoy.

2. Plans for your next date.

3. The effect a public event has on the two of you.

4. Your impressions of each other when you first met.

5. How your career goals interrelate with his.

ACCENTUATE THE POSITIVE

Present yourself in the best possible light. There are times when you need to brag, to make self-serving statements such as "I was the smartest student in math class" or "I've been told many times that I have lovely hair." If you want the man to believe that you are beautiful and intelligent, you have to show him that you believe in yourself.

Place pleasant thoughts about yourself into conversations with him whenever you can. If he compliments you, thank him, but reinforce the compliment by repeating it as well. If he says that you are pretty, for instance, say "I'm glad you think I'm pretty." As soon as one positive idea about you reaches him, create another. Bombard him with positive thoughts. Let him *know* that you're a treasure!

Make sure your assertions are reasonable, however. If you claim that you are Princess Jasmine, the daughter of the Royal House of Solomon, no man will believe you. Show him your good qualities, but don't exaggerate them, and never resort to lying. These statements are not only worthless, the man will hold them against you.

WHAT ABOUT YOUR WEAKNESSES?

Do you have a birthmark or a more serious physical defect? If so, some of the men you have dated may have avoided the topic in order to spare your feelings. If they did mention the flaw, you might have asked them not to mention it again. But whether your weakness is a wart on your nose, a limp, or fifty extra pounds, it will not go away because it is unmentioned. Instead, pretending the defect does not exist isolates the two of you from each other.

Do mention your obvious defects, but don't do it in a way that is designed to elicit sympathy. It's better to say "Did you ever see such a scar?" than to pretend that the scar does not exist. But wait until you and he are interested in each other before you bring this defect up.

At the same time, though, do not go to the other

extreme and dwell on your defects. That is an even worse mistake. He can see the physical imperfections, whether it's a flat chest, big nose, poor skin, unruly hair, or crooked teeth. If you feel strong about your defects and must purge yourself with a confession, confess to your parents or relatives, or to friends whom you are not planning to wed.

Avoiding a Negative Image

A man needs an association with a woman with whom he can forget his own mental conflicts. He's looking for a friend and a companion in sex, not someone who insists on frequently reciting her personal medical history, her fears about money, and her physical and mental deficiencies. If you load the man down with undesirable images about yourself, it will ultimately lead to your rejection.

If you went out to buy an automobile and the saleman kept reminding you that the car could get flat tires, that the radiator might leak, that the transmission could break down, and that the upholstery will probably fade, you would find another salesman, even if you liked the car!

Some women boast about their poor health, poor vision, allergies, lack of stamina, or broken-down arches as if these deficiencies were attributes. Even if a man admires daintiness (and many do not), he will not view frailty as a virtue.

In addition, the man may intensify any statements you make against yourself. If a woman says "I am an unworthy soul, a wretched person, ignorant, ugly, and decrepit" and so on, the man is likely to believe her even if these things are not true. Present yourself honestly, but emphasize the positive.

Eventually, if the relationship becomes serious and progresses toward marriage, you and your man should discuss such topics as your sexual needs, your financial liabilities, and the relatives for whom you are responsible. But wait for the relationship to develop before having these discussions, and don't dwell on your own weaknesses along the way.

WATCH WHAT YOU SAY

There are eight subject areas that require special handling in the developing stages of a relationship:

1. RELIGION AND ETHNIC GROUP. Do not attempt to convert the male to your religion; nor should you be chauvinistic about your ethnic group. If either have anything to offer, your example will convey it.

2. SURVIVAL. Unless the facts are otherwise, let him know that you are capable of supporting yourself. If you are really in economic stress, show him that you can "grin and bear it."

3. TALKING DIRTY. Sometimes a woman will use dirty words when she is with a man in an attempt to appear down-to-earth. The result, however, may be quite the contrary, especially if the man is older and more traditional. Such a man will visualize the word, and the woman will be degraded in his mind. Know your audience, and avoid these consequences! Wait until he uses these words first.

4. SOUNDING CHILDISH. Many women are passed by for marriage because they do not speak like mature adults. Even though they wouldn't consider dressing for a date in diapers, or arranging their hair in pigtails, their discussions with a man may be loaded with immature nonsense and girlish giggles. Please, if you're old enough to read this material, don't giggle!

5. PSEUDO-SCIENCES. When did you last see a horoscope in a men's magazine? Very few men believe in astrology, fortune-telling, or reincarnation. If you believe in such things, realize that a lot of men are likely to hold these beliefs against you.

6. IRRATIONAL FEARS. Displays of fear that are not founded on good reason are harmful to your relationship with men. We are all familiar with the cartoon of the fat lady perched on a chair because a tiny mouse is scurrying across her kitchen floor. Do not shriek at the sight of a bug or a mouse; your man will lose respect for you. A man will view you very negatively if you act squeamish at the sight of blood. He will think you are incapable of taking care of him if he becomes sick or injured. Once he reaches this conclusion, he is likely to pass you by as a potential mate. Irrational fears may be held against you, whether it's a fear of moving out of your neighborhood or a fear of elevators.

7. DON'T SOUND LIKE A PARASITE. Some women act like parasites. They tell their friends, only partially in jest, that it would be great to have a rich old man with one foot in the grave and the other on a banana peel. This idea is repulsive to men. If you are not a parasite, don't sound like one.

A woman who is not parasitical may inadvertently

give such an impression by talking about how she dislikes work, enjoys elaborate vacations, desires travel, and loves clothing and jewelry. She may brag that she is unable to cook or entertain herself. Then she wonders why men pass her by for marriage.

Don't let such careless statements keep you from marriage. Think about what you say, and avoid statements that may make you sound parasitical.

8. DON'T SOUND LIKE A PROSTITUTE. Some women demand expensive gifts because they are unwilling to "sell themselves cheaply." They are afraid to give something away, namely themselves, without sufficient payment. But if you expect the man to pay for the pleasure of your company, he is likely to see you as a prostitute rather than a future wife.

Don't ask for gifts or ask the man to spend money on you. Don't even hint. If he offers you an expensive gift, accept it only if you tell him he can have it back. A man who finds a truly considerate woman will eventually be generous, but no man wants to believe that he must spend great sums to enjoy good female companionship.

ANGER AND ARGUMENTS

Arguments will happen, even with the man you love, though if you can handle these arguments appropriately, you will enhance his respect for you. An argument that is not nipped in the bud with logical responses and self-control can end up in a fight. Learn to argue without fighting. Try to resolve your disagreements before you reach the point of anger. Otherwise, it may be too late.

To succeed with your man when he is angry, let him displace his anger. Make sure there is something minor he can yell about. For example, leave part of your closet a mess. Your man won't complain about the slight mess, except when he's in a bad mood. The messy closet area is a "safety valve" that helps him to blow off steam. Think of other displacement ideas that will work for you.

Anger is sometimes justified. When it is, it may need to be expressed. Let him vent his angers that are not directed toward you. Become aware of his angers and recognize his need for release. Let him rant and rave. You do not want his anger toward others to keep him from marriage with you. Be emotionally prepared so you are not affected by what he says in anger and do not become angry yourself or feel hurt by his complaints.

You and he may get angry at each other from time to time. This type of anger is natural as long as it isn't frequent. The maximum frequency for anger depends on your upbringing and his; people from angry households usually have a greater tolerance for anger.

Be aware of the difference between crankiness and anger. Pay more attention to the anger that your man expresses after dinner than before!

Some arguments with your man will make you so angry that your behavior toward him will be affected. You may not want to talk to him, go out with him, or sleep with him. If you must, withhold other things, but never deny sex because of anger. This denial of sex weakens sexual exclusivity; if he's in need of sexual satisfaction he may find it elsewhere.

An angry person often behaves in either a hostile or indifferent manner. Your angry behavior can destroy your relationship if it is emotionally painful to the man, costs him money, or causes him a loss of self-respect. If you are angry to the point that you can't behave rationally with your companion, then blow off your anger by telling someone, such as a close friend, what is troubling you.

After you vent your anger, you may be able to regain self-control. If "venting" does not help and you feel like trampling your man, then postpone seeing him for a week. But set down a definite time to meet with him or you may never see him again. Seven days without you may lead him into someone else's arms. If you are still filled with anger a week later, your relationship is probably over.

Pride causes havoc in male–female relationships because it sustains anger. Excessive pride is one of the primary reasons that relationships end. When you feel insulted by your man, you may want satisfaction through either a humble apology or an end to the relationship. Women sometimes make such statements as "He is not going to talk to me that way" and "I'm not going to let him get away with that!" This attitude is the beginning of the end of a relationship. You may be faced with the choice of letting go of your pride and keeping the man or of letting go of the man and keeping your pride.

Fighting is a sign that one party (if not both) is unhappy with the relationship. Usually "fighting" couples end up parting, and each person has lost time on misspent emotions. Do not waste your time fighting! If you are fighting frequently, take the difficult step of ending the relationship.

CHAPTER 8

Praising and Criticizing the One You Love

Many women believe that they can snare a man by using beauty, cooking, social standing, sex, or wealth, but there is a far better strategy. Act like his wife and treat him like your husband. How? By praising and criticizing him.

Praise and criticism generate the intense emotions that enable a relationship to develop. Equally important, praise and criticism are expected as part of everyday family life, particularly in relationships between husband and wife.

Your parents loved you, but they criticized. They said "Your room is a mess" or "You can't come to the dinner table until you comb your hair" or "If you are so smart, why did you get only a B in English?" Because of your upbringing, you associate a certain level of criticism with love.

The man's parents made him feel special, loved, and in a class by himself. They referred to him as "our precious child," yet they were always pointing out his imperfections. This is a pattern of behavior you can follow and use to your advantage.

Praise the man to make him feel special. Your recognition of his uniqueness should be the reason you want to provide him with your companionship, with sex, with everything you have to offer. But you must also criticize the one you love, or you will ultimately lose out. Criticism intensifies the relationship because it stirs the man's emotions. When you balance criticism with praise, the net effect is stronger positive emotions felt toward you.

Let's begin with praise, because most men require more praise than criticism. Praise him first, to make sure he is emotionally strong enough to withstand the criticism you'll be handing out later. Don't lie, however. If you do not really find him unique, you should have eliminated him previously from further consideration as a prospective mate. It's not too late. If you can't praise him without lying, don't praise him at all. Say good-bye instead.

THE NEED FOR PRAISE

A man needs to feel special in order to be happy, and he looks to a woman to tell him that he is special. His male friends don't reinforce those feelings because they are too preoccupied with their own sense of uniqueness.

Make Him Feel Unique

The man's need to be unique may cause him to insist on a by-line or screen credit, drive an unusual automobile, join a country club instead of using public parks, participate in exotic sports, tell outrageous stories, wear expensive jewelry and only certain clothing, overspend, tip outrageously, live only in certain areas, or do anything that he thinks is beyond what the ordinary man would do. Listen to men's conversations the next time you attend a gathering; each tells stories of his cleverness, of how he outwitted someone else.

Ask your man "When did you first realize that you were unique?" You may be amazed at his answer. He may have felt "different" since he was four or five! The more intelligent the man, the earlier he felt unique. He may even remember the specific circumstances when he realized his uniqueness.

Encourage the man to tell you how different he is from other men. Ask him about his excellence in his job, his conversations with his boss or clients, the honors or praise he's received in his occupation or in school, and how superior he is to others around him.

Emphasize the characteristics of his personality that you or he believe demonstrate his uniqueness. Smile or nod with approval over any story that shows his superiority over the next person. Listening, adding your approval to what you hear, and telling him how unique he is are the easiest ways of pleasing him.

Be a clever woman and tell your man "You are unique," "You are so different from other men," "There's something special about you." You'll gain his love as you reinforce his concept of his being special. He becomes addicted to your praise, especially when you mix it with criticism, because he will recognize that your praise is genuine.

Uniqueness can also be attained by being the "most" or the "best" in anything. Tell your man that he is the most intelligent, most creative, most precious, most unusual, most interesting, most fun, most ambitious person you know. Use whatever adjective you think will be pleasing, effective, and uncommon.

Positive and Negative Thoughts

A man wants to believe that he is different, but from time to time, he recognizes that he is just an ordinary man. When he dwells on the negative, he also recalls that any joy or talent he has is very temporary, and that the end result of life is death.

Most men, even under the most ideal conditions, face a hostile world. Since each man needs to feel unique to combat his negative thoughts, he attempts to diminish the next person's importance. A man wants a woman who helps him combat his negative thoughts with her praise.

Negative statements are more intense than positive ones. If someone walked up to you and said, "You are very beautiful," you would soon forget the compliment. But if someone said, "You have a big nose," you would not soon forget it. You probably receive more praise than criticism, but you remember the criticism more vividly. So does a man. If you give praise effectively, you will attract men. Each will develop feelings of gratitude and affection for you.

How to Praise Effectively

Always greet your man by name and with a warm hello. Let him know with your smile that you're happy to see him. Mention his name about once every two to ten minutes when you're chatting. The sound of his name may be his favorite sound, so use his name frequently.

Since you want your man to be very happy with you, continue caressing him with words. Tell him that you find him physically attractive and appreciate his good mind. Again, if you can't do this honestly, find someone else.

Start with his physical attributes. Tell him that he is

handsome, that his glances are exciting to you, that his muscles are strong. Compliment him on many of his features so he knows that you desire him. If any features are outstanding, give them great emphasis. If his looks are less than average, try to tell him that although he may not meet the concept of "attractive" for some women, he is sufficiently attractive to you.

Next, praise his thinking! Validate his thoughts by telling him he is intelligent. If you do not agree with his conclusions, say so, but acknowledge that he uses good logic. (Of course, it is possible to over-sweeten. There are remedies for over-sweetening, but rarely are there remedial measures for sourness.)

Your man needs to know what you think of him. Your statements are important because he is affected by the attitudes of others. He cannot see himself and cannot evaluate himself with certainty, so he depends on feedback.

He cannot approach someone and say to them "Tell me, how do I appear to you? Am I attractive? The sensuous type? Do I look intelligent?" and "Am I sexually desirable?" You can set yourself up as a mirror, reflecting for him how he appears to the world. He might be taken aback or amused at first, but he will be an ardent listener and will want to hear more. Your ease in showing him to himself will let him know that you are self-assured enough to evaluate him.

Make Him Feel Important

Sally, a single woman, was busy telling me that she knew nothing about making a man feel important when a neighborhood youngster, about six years old, dashed into her kitchen. Her eyes sparkled when she saw this boy. She hugged him, fondled his hair, offered him the seat next to her, and gave him milk and cookies. She listened to him tell her what he had being doing that day and showed enthusiasm and interest in him. She made him feel that he was important to her.

Most women have no trouble making a six-year-old boy feel important. Remember that your man, even if he is six feet four and thirty-six years old, is still a six-year-old at heart.

Jane was a corporate executive with a limited social life. She was frightened by the thought of talking to her dates, although she felt comfortable with people up and down the corporate ladder. While Jane was thinking about how difficult it was for her to communicate with men on a dating level, Jim, one of her key staff members, walked into her office for his weekly chat.

Jane sat Jim down and made sure he was reasonably comfortable. She offered him refreshments and the opportunity to discuss anything that was on his mind concerning the business. She listened to him intensely, made mental notes about his positive contributions, and then reiterated his success stories with enthusiasm and interest in her voice. Jane made her staff member feel important. Once she transferred her talent for listening and praising to her social life, she became highly desirable.

THE NEED FOR CRITICISM

Early in your relationship, you and your date are both likely to be on your best behavior. Yet over the long run you both will be uncomfortable if you must remain on your best behavior all the time. You need to relax and become comfortable with each other. A certain level of criticism can ease the transition from formal behavior to relaxed informality. Use criticism to nudge him off his pedestal. He does not enjoy pretending to be perfect any more than you do.

If you tactfully criticize the man you love, he will be pleased with your attention, because he recognizes that criticism is quite different from rejection. You can, and should, criticize him, but always do so with acceptance of him. He will enjoy knowing that you recognize that he is a mere earthling and that you love him anyway.

When "polite" conversation becomes boring, then it's time to open up new topics. Surely you've figured out what areas he may feel sensitive about. Bring up one of those areas and let him know that your fondness or respect for him is not diminished by it. Say to him, "Ben, you're a little short but very darling. I imagine you sometimes wished you were taller?" He may welcome the invitation to express some of his frustrations over his height or pride in overcoming feelings of inferiority about it.

If your man has delusions of personal grandeur that shut you out or diminish your worth, you can, by criticizing him, build yourself up. Never let him think he is too good for you.

Criticize in Private

One grave error a woman can make is to criticize her man in front of others. Men hate to be wrong in public, even when the situation is unimportant. When a woman purchases something from a store and later decides that she doesn't want the item, she does not hesitate to return it. Men, however, rarely return any item they've bought unless it's defective. Since men hate to be wrong in public when the situation is unimportant, they detest being wrong in public when the situation is important.

Don't forget the criticism; simply delay airing it until the two of you are alone.

Distinguishing Criticisms and Insults

Criticize the man, but do not insult him or physically abuse him. There is a big difference between criticism and insults, and this distinction is crucial when you love someone.

Criticisms point out faults, while insults are rude remarks whose purpose is only to anger. When you are insulted, you respond to the vehemence of the speaker, not the substance of the statement. When you are criticized, you focus on the substance of what is said. If a statement is both an insult and a criticism, you respond to both what was said *and* the vehemence with which it was said.

Suppose you are in the supermarket check-out line. Another woman accuses you of trying to sneak ahead of her. She calls you a fat, pushy, overbearing, loudmouth slob. These statements are insults, attempts to belittle and anger you.

Suppose, however, that the woman said that you were sneaking ahead to avoid having people see you in your tattered dress, or that you cut in front of her because you are too nearsighted to see what you were doing. These statements may be insults, but if your dress is old or you are nearsighted, they are also criticisms because they point out actual faults. Even if you do not feel a sting at the moment you are criticized, these thoughts remain in your mind and you may feel the sting of criticism in time.

Use noninsulting criticisms with your man: "It's a good thing you think better than you spell." "Can't you

see that tie doesn't match? Put on the blue one." These
criticisms will not cause a normal man to flee from you.
Criticism has an important role in your relationship with
men, but insults do not.

USING HIS FEELINGS OF INFERIORITY

Every man has parts of himself he feels superior
about and parts he feels inferior about. You want him
because of his superior attributes, but you will succeed
with him because of his weaknesses. The key to a successful relationship is to know his inferiorities, so you can
determine how and when to criticize him once you have
praised him.

The man will talk about his superiorities, but
uncovering his inferiorities is more difficult. When you
meet a man, it is as if he is wearing a suit of armor. He is
hiding his innermost thoughts and conflicts, his passions
and desires, and his feelings of inferiority. Pierce the
facade that he shows to the public.

When you interview him, look for the five most
common and devastating inferiorities men feel: origin-
based, physical, financial, mental, and moral. Discover
these feelings early in the relationship, and keep them in
mind when you consider whether he is the right man for
you. Use them when it becomes necessary to criticize
him.

Many men will talk freely about their feelings of
inferiority with someone who approaches the subject
empathetically and appears intelligent. As he talks about
his weaknesses and failures, he will become very comfortable with you, and you will become very knowledgeable
about him.

Origin-Based

A man may feel inferior about his origin or birth, including ethnic background, religion, race, appearance of family members, jobs, schools attended, or home where he grew up. When you ask a man "Where did you come from?" or "What does your father do?" or "Where were you born?" he may worry that you think he is from a Third World country, a shack, or a poor neighborhood.

If a man brags about his ancestry, don't let him look only to his illustrious ancestors and exclude the rest. During the past 400 years, each of us had more than 100,000 direct ancestors, excluding the effects of inter-breeding. If you could trace his ancestry back to these 100,000 ancestors, you are likely to find unsavory characters of various types. When he mentions one ancestor, ask him why he excluded the others. You might not be able to call him a son of a bitch, but you might be able to call him a great-great-great-grandson of a bitch.

What should you do if the man criticizes your origins? Beam with pride that you have overcome any inferiority associated with a lowly background!

Physical

A man may feel physically inferior because of actual inadequacies, lack of physical acceptance by others, or because he is uncomfortable with his own body. He may be concerned that he is the wrong height, is unattractive, has poor vision or crooked teeth, or is too young or too old. Even a handsome man winces at any references to his size, age, weight, shape, build, hair, or dress.

The man's appearance is an especially good source of criticism because we do not see ourselves except as a reflection in a mirror, and this sight we usually scorn.

What should you do if the man criticizes *your* appearance? Unless your inadequacies are extremely apparent, let him know that many men find you attractive and that the feature he sees as a flaw is considered an attribute by others. Let him know that there is no universal beauty, and that you are more beautiful than Miss Universe to some men.

Financial

A man may attempt to diminish you by bragging about his wealth or income. If he does, bring him down to size by provoking his own feelings of financial inferiority. You might say, "You're so smart, I'm surprised you're not richer." Comment on the low financial return he receives on his assets, or their slow appreciation in value, or the excessive amount of taxes he pays.

Even a very wealthy man is familiar with super-wealth and will feel an inferiority about his worth. Most men compare themselves to the richest man they know, never making comparisons to the less fortunate. If John owns a hotel, he compares himself to Nicky, who owns three hotels, while Nicky compares himself with Ron, who owns a large hotel chain.

A man who is hovering about the poverty line may cringe when you ask him what kind of car he drives, or where he bought his shirt, or where he lives. If he is poor, only evoke his feelings of financial inferiority in self-defense.

Education

Even a well-educated man knows that there is much he does not know. Men are always concerned about being asked a question in public that they should know the answer to but don't. A man rarely feels adequate outside his field. Even in his field he may not feel fully confident, since he may not know the sub-specialties. Never let him think he is too bright for you.

Ethics

A man may be concerned with his ethics and those of his family. He may have secrets that would embarrass him profoundly if the public found them out. He may question whether his family has clean hands in achieving their present position in society. Did his father make shady deals? Is his brother on drugs? Is there an illegitimate child in the family? Use his sense of moral inferiority if he is attacking your morals or ethics, but use this kind of criticism for self-defense only.

Other Inferiorities

You can make the man conscious of such inferiorities as inadequate social skills, lack of status, low self-esteem, lack of accomplishments, and so on. When you criticize the man, attack him on any inferiority you wish, as long as you do not remove his feeling of uniqueness, challenge his zeniths, attack his sexuality, or criticize him in public— these four approaches are too severe to be used if you want to continue your relationship.

The Man's Feelings of Inferiority Are Stronger

Every person suffers from feelings of inferiority, but men usually suffer more than women. You will have greater self-confidence in dealing with men when you understand why.

Men typically have greater feelings of inferiority than women do because men compare themselves unfavorably with other men. A man may compare himself adversely as to his physical, mental, moral, financial, and familial attributes to those of the best man he knows in each category.

Men take jabs at each other rather than being supportive. A bald man may be affectionately referred to by his male friends as "Melonhead." Women friends would not tease one another in this way.

When a woman compares herself to another woman, she balances the good and the bad. A woman may think, "Well, she's richer, but I'm younger." The woman is kinder to herself in self-judgments.

When He Is Arrogant

If you need to, you can highlight any and all of a man's inferiorities. This is the technique to use when he is particularly arrogant, especially if he sharpens his tone of voice in speaking to you, challenges your uniqueness and importance, or becomes overly critical and picky. You can also use this technique if he starts taking you for granted or shows any signs of boredom with you. At those times, criticize. You need to build yourself up! On occasion, you can ridicule him with such sarcastic remarks as "Sure, you are Mister Universe" or "Yes, I remember when you received an Oscar." Statements such as these can be used to revive his feelings of inferiority without frightening him away.

It is regrettable that you must build yourself up by tearing the other person down, but you can never let him think he is too good for you. Diminish his importance if he is trying to diminish yours.

If he brags that he is wealthy—but only if he brags—tell him about people who are wealthier. If he is a capitalist, tell him he thinks too much like a socialist. If he is a doctor, tell him that he acts like a waiter. Make such comments as "You may be a professional, but you sure don't speak like one" or "If you were two inches taller, you'd be perfect" or "Your clothes almost match."

Many women who are conscious of their own inferiorities are afraid to criticize a man. The idea behind the popular expression "People who live in glass houses shouldn't throw stones" keeps them quiet. They fear that the men will turn on them and devastate what little pride they have. When you incite a man's inferiorities to the extent that they hurt him, he will retaliate with nasty words of his own. Expect this natural reaction and realize it means that you have reached him. He may not mean the things he says when he is hurt; it's his way of saying "Ouch!"

Do not carry your use of negative statements to extremes, though. If the man becomes convinced that you are out to destroy his ego, he will turn on you. You cannot push him into a situation where the survival of his self-importance is at issue. Even your own pet puppy dog will withstand your spanking only as long as it feels you are not planning its destruction.

USING THE MAN'S CONSCIENCE

When you need to criticize a man, you can use his conscience as a basis for this criticism. If he acts haughty or aloof, this technique will bring him down to earth. His conscience was influenced by various individuals, living or dead. They influenced his moral values and his views of himself, and he feels that he must account to them in some way. He attempts to act in a manner that pleases them even at the expense of his own happiness.

The man's conscience is affected most by his parents, bosses, spouses, relatives, friends, clergy, teachers, and enemies. Answer these questions to determine who is affecting your man.

1. Who is he not "himself" with?
2. Who censors his ideas and conversations?
3. For whom does he dress?
4. From whom would he hide his emotional conflicts?
5. Who would be concerned if he brought home a woman of a different religion or national origin?
6. For whom does he tidy up his home more than usual?
7. Who would be disappointed to see him poorly groomed?
8. From whom does he hide his true financial position?
9. Who are the people he would not ask for a loan even if he were starving?
10. From whom would he hide his sexual history?

Listen to your man carefully and determine who is on his list. Then, when you need to diminish him, bring up the unpleasant thoughts these people create. The following examples show how you could make use of a man's conscience:

1. "What would your mother say if she saw you acting like this?"

2. "Does your boss know how little you know about that?"

3. "Would your sister think as much of you if she knew you lost that client?"

4. "Wouldn't Jerry like to know how little money you really made last month?"

The individuals who formed your man's conscience make him feel disappointing to them and to himself. They create in him a sense of inferiority or inadequacy.

BALANCE PRAISE AND CRITICISM

During many of your conversations, you enhance or diminish the other person. This happens naturally as part of the "battle of the sexes," or even when you are with a friend or colleague of the same sex. In the course of an evening, you might make twenty positive comments and eight negative ones. This is the salt and pepper of conversation. By combining praise with criticism, you are saying, "I am good enough for you, but are you good enough for me?" It's important, however, to maintain the proper balance.

If you were a movie critic and claimed to like every

film you reviewed, the public would lose respect for you. If you condemned every film, you would also lose credibility. To show that you have a discerning mind, you need to use both praise and criticism. You couldn't be an effective parent, teacher, executive, coach, or spouse without knowing how to balance praise and criticism.

Always praise your man in front of his immediate family, co-workers, and friends. Be his advocate and speak well of him to these individuals. Make comments such as "If anyone can do it, he can!" However, if you feel that your praise will inflate his ego, then remove the praise privately. A comment such as "Your boss really believed everything I said about you" will suffice.

There are more criticizing or negative adjectives in the English language than there are praising or positive ones. The ratio is almost three to one. Therefore, you probably use adjectives in that same ratio. Stop that bad habit and start using a balance that will further your relationship.

The proper balance of praise and criticism is rarely fifty-fifty. Most men will only be comfortable if praise exceeds criticism by a ratio of three or four to one. You must discover your man's own needs.

During your interviewing, determine how much praise and criticism your man received during his early years, as a teenager, and as an adult. Most men view their family with fondness and are comfortable with the balance of praise and criticism they had growing up. For those men who rebelled against the level of praise and criticism they received when they were younger, don't base your treatment of them on prior experiences. Determine their need for praise and criticism based on later successful interpersonal experiences in adulthood.

A person is most likely to rebel against the praise and criticism he received if the praise-criticism ratio was skewed too greatly in one direction or the other. If the criticism he received greatly exceeded the praise he received, your man may have been a victim of child abuse. On the other hand, if the praise exceeded the criticism by a vast margin, he may have felt that he could not live up to the expectations people had for him. In either event he is likely to be an angry man and you should be careful not to repeat his past pattern.

You may need to change your behavior to win his love. Are you a dud, who says nothing; a fan, who praises and doesn't criticize; a nag, who criticizes and doesn't praise; or a bitch, who does both? Of these four alternatives, bitchiness is the best; it keeps the man's emotions alive and makes him seek out your praise.

The Dud

If you never praise or criticize the man, he will view you as a dud. You may think of refraining from criticism as politeness or kindness, but he will see it as a weakness. If you never criticize him, he is likely to be thinking one of three things:

1. You are too dumb to recognize his faults, and therefore are too dumb for him.

2. You are too insecure to point out his faults, and therefore are too cowardly for him.

3. He really is perfect, in which case he is certainly too good for you.

The Fan

We were taught to be nice, to not say unpleasant things, so that others would like us. "If you don't have something nice to say, don't say anything." Niceness gets little children a pat on the head by their parents or teachers, but doesn't get a man to love us, need us, and marry us. Put aside the childish rule of "niceness" and undertake conversations that incite a man's curiosity, passion, and desire. Do not fawn over him or act like a fan. If you are too nice, you will eventually be taken for granted and your man will have the same thoughts about you that he has about the dud.

The Nag

The nag loses out by constantly criticizing the man. If you criticize him more than his mother did, you are looking for trouble.

The Bitch

Think of the women you know who are most success-ful with men. These are the women who are demanding and complain to their men, but accept them nonetheless. You may think of these women as bitchy, but they have men flocking around them, men you lost by being nice. You may sometimes need to act bitchy to succeed with men.

Let your man know that you have a high self-esteem. Most men respond favorably to a woman who is hard to please if she selects him. The man is honored to marry her! The man's thought process will be as follows:

1. She has a high opinion of herself.
2. Therefore, she must be someone special.
3. She has a low opinion of most people.
4. Therefore, if she accepts *me* as her man, I must be someone special!

The phenomenon of men rejecting the "nice woman" is shocking to most women. However, women constantly reject men who are always kind to them. Women view extreme kindness in men as a weakness, and label these men wimps.

The difference between the bitch, who succeeds with men, and the nag, who loses men, is that the bitch succeeds by alternately accepting the man—telling him he is wonderful and making a fuss over him—and dumping on him for his faults. Occasional bitching will keep them coming back for more, but constant nagging will lead to failure. Be a bitch, not a nag!

WHEN HE CRITICIZES YOU

It is usually the man who makes the woman feel inferior, and his comments can really hurt you. What should you do when a man points out your inferiorities or criticizes you? Learn not to show your emotions. Don't allow anyone to push you into reactions with either criticism or praise. Stay in the middle emotionally if you can.

When a man puts you down, ask him "Is that all?" Repeat that question until he says yes. Then diminish him in a manner comparable to his tirade against you.

Conclude with a general acceptance of him, such as "In spite of your childish antics, I'm stuck on you." Soon, you'll teach him to vent his angers and forget them!

When you know you are going to lose your cool, try this strategy: Show your anger, but don't let him know what really caused the hurt. This is the safest approach for your own psyche, since if he knows exactly what reached you, he can cause you real pain any time. As you gain experience, though, it will become easier to control your own behavior.

CHAPTER 9

Developing Your Sexual Strategy

You are meeting between a hundred and a thousand men to find your ideal mate, so don't begin sex with a man until you have interviewed and approved him and he has invested emotions in you. Make sure he is within that five or ten percent you are considering as a potential spouse. Then, make sure the timing is right. If you either have sex too soon or delay too long, you will lose the man for marriage.

Not long ago, a young woman told me that she had had sex with hundreds of men, but none of these relationships had resulted in marriage. Sex without a commitment is possible, but it is the wrong way to lead the man of your choice to marriage. If you have sex with a stranger, he may well remain a stranger. Casual sex is dead, at least for a woman seeking marriage.

Another woman told me that she has been "saving herself" for marriage, viewing her continued virginity as an asset of increasing value. She had also failed with men. You should be looking for and expecting sex as part of your relationship. If sex does not begin after a while, something is wrong.

Both of these extreme sexual strategies are likely to fail. Let's focus on how sex can lead to marriage.

BEGINNING THE SEXUAL RELATIONSHIP

As an adult woman, you know about the female sex drive, but you might not know how important sex is to men. In fact, sex is a predominant thought in the mind of a normal man, second only to self-preservation. If the man does not have to worry about his survival, he thinks about satisfying his sexual needs.

For both males and females, the sex drive is an urge that has to be satisfied for the person to be physically comfortable. Sex is a need that requires fulfillment; a person in need of sex is likely to be irritable and fearful. With each continuing day of no relief, sexual tensions increase and the person becomes incapable of relaxing or concentrating.

Some women claim that men want relationships with them only for sex. In fact, men want much more, and while most men will not stay with a woman who offers little or no sex, sex alone is not enough.

Sex as Recognition

When you have sex with a man who believes that you are sexually selective, you are indicating to him that he is special. Tell him that you are hard to impress, but that he has succeeded. Make your sexual selectivity a form of recognition.

Sexual performance is also a form of recognition.

However, a woman will be more successful at the beginning of a relationship by giving a man recognition in other ways. Men with high sex drives will respond more favorably to early sexual recognition than will other men.

If a man believes that a woman finds him desirable, he will not end a relationship with her solely because she delays sex for a while. The nonsexual beginning, from minutes to years, depends on the man's mores and sex drive.

Moral Code

If you want a man for marriage, you must follow his moral code. If you cannot do so without violating your own, move on and find someone who is more compatible.

If you transgress his code, the man will pass you by for marriage. For example, if you have anal sex with a man before you know his sexual standards, and he really disapproves of anal sex, he may consciously enjoy the performance while subconsciously holding the act against you.

Determine a man's background and how far he deviates from it. Questions such as "Did your parents indulge in premarital sex?" or "Is your sister a virgin?" or "Did you ever see your parents in the nude?" are keys to his sexual values. If he recoils in horror just from your merely asking these questions, you can be sure that he is mired in prudery. If he has an adult unmarried daughter, or a widowed mother, find out how he feels about her sexual activity. If he would say "no sex" for her, you should say "no sex" to him, since he has traditional, antisexual values.

Play it safe by consenting only to sex acts that are generally acceptable. Place the burden of any deviation upon him. For example, if he asks for anal sex, let him be the one to convince you that it is natural or proper.

Judge your man by what he does, not by what he says he does. If you have listened to him speak without restraint, you should be able to predict with great probability what you must do to make him react favorably to you.

When to Start Sex

Sex is a natural consequence of a male–female relationship. However, since sex is the greatest gift you may offer a man, you must carefully build it up beyond other natural pleasures to have it work to your advantage. A man, however, also views his sexual activity as the greatest gift he can offer. If you reject sex with him, he may look for someone else.

Sex should begin when there is both curiosity and affection. Give the man sufficient chance to develop sexual curiosity about you, since curiosity can normally sustain a relationship for about ten sexual encounters. But more than curiosity is needed over the long term, so make sure that the man develops deep affection for you as well. You must build the relationship before having sex; this is your assurance that he won't leave you after he satisfies his sexual curiosity. Wait until the man's anticipation of enjoying sex with you is so great that the occasion will be like a national holiday. But remember, holidays come and go. Don't postpone sex too long or the relationship is likely to wither and die.

As a rule of thumb, have approximately a dozen dates with a man before you have sex. Assuming you are contemplating marriage to him, make sure that these dates have included at least thirty hours of conversation between the two of you.

It is sometimes to a woman's advantage to postpone the sexual relationship even longer. If a man has old-fashioned values, and was on the losing side in the sexual revolution, continue the delay if you can comfortably forgo sex. The longer he waits, the greater value he will place on the initial sex act.

AIDS is causing a growing concern. Know a man well before you have sex with him to make sure he is a safe sex partner. Men too are seeking safe sex partners. If you insist that your man use condoms until you both are sure you can't infect each other, he should appreciate your caution and selectivity, and raise his esteem of you as a wife.

How to Delay Sex

When the man makes advances to you and you want to delay sex, do not tease him or incite his passions. If he becomes too aroused and is not satisfied, he may be angry with you for teasing him to that point. To keep your man coming back to see you before you are having sex with him, indicate that you will have sex with him as soon as you know him better. Tell him that you like him physically, but do not want to rush into a sexual relationship.

Reject having sex, but not him. You can say something like the following: "Every man I've dated wanted to take me to bed. What kind of wife would I make for you or any man if I had always allowed it?" Furthermore, the man will usually believe that as you act with him, you have acted with others.

These approaches should restrain him long enough to build his desires. When he is so eager for you that you feel he cannot stop, that's the point at which you should go to bed with him.

Once Sex Begins

Make the first sexual experience with your prospective husband as intense and as unforgettable as possible. Once sex begins, the man will compare the woman to others he has slept with. This comparison is often favorable, but it can be harsh. The woman may be passed by for marriage by an old-fashioned man merely for having sex too early, or by a more modern man who views her performance as poor.

Most men want to marry a woman who is sexually competent, a woman who is "good in bed." The typical man reacts adversely to virginity in an adult female, but he does not seek a woman with great sexual expertise. To increase you marriageability, avoid these two extremes. Develop your sexual competency without becoming a "sexpert."

The Virgin

A man usually does not appreciate virginity in an adult female any more than he admires a woman who doesn't drive a car, read, or swim. He desires competence from a woman in all these activities and many others.

If, at the outset of a sexual encounter, an adult woman tells her man that she is a virgin, he is likely to wonder why no man has wanted her before. If this is your situation, let him know that other men have wanted you, but that he is unique in being able to have you. This technique has its limitations, particularly if you are past your twenties, since most men recognize that there are limits to their uniqueness. Most women find an adult male strange if he has never had sex. Men normally view virginity in an adult female with equal dismay. If a woman is a virgin and over twenty-five, and insists on remaining a virgin until she marries, she is likely to die a virgin.

The Sexpert

The "sexpert," the woman with sexual expertise, is often frightening to men. If you know a thousand and one positions and have used them all, keep this knowledge to yourself, at least in the beginning of a relationship. A man typically wants to believe that his knowledge of sex is at least as great as his woman's.

ENHANCING SEX

Make your bed an adult playpen. Create an atmosphere that is relaxed, sensual, and inviting so that your man knows you are anticipating him with joy.

Some clothing is more erotic than none at all, so excite him with various stages of dress and undress. A gesture such as loosening his tie, slipping off his shoes, or unbuttoning his shirt will create a positive mood. Make the removal of clothing a playful art. Comment on how you enjoy his hairy chest, or strong arms, or big hands. Sexual teasing is appropriate now because it is going to lead to sexual satisfaction.

And, of course, the best way to arouse a man is

to be aroused yourself. Your feelings will be contagious. Plant the idea of sex in your man's mind early in the day. That way, when he sees you in the evening, his desire for you will have been long awakened. Expressions such as "Honey, I can hardly wait to enjoy you" will spark him. Keep him in anticipation for a few hours. His passions will be greater, and he will find you to be especially desirable.

On rare occasions, you can enhance a sexual encounter by evoking anger, but not furor, before the sex act. You've probably heard of couples who have terrible fights and then make up and have the best sex ever. If you incite one sense, you may awaken the others. If you tease the man to anger, you may arouse him sexually as well. He will believe that there is something special about his passions for you. Do not use this technique except in rare instances, though, because the fight could get out of control.

Sexual mechanics do not vary much from person to person. However, you can be very different from other women both before and after the sex act by establishing a pleasurable ambiance. Use everything at your disposal to enhance the moment. If you usually have sex in your home, buy a robe or lounging outfit for him to wear whenever he's there. Provide him with his favorite toiletries. Use music, dim lights, and an inviting room to create warm and comfortable feelings.

Sexual Cycle and Compatibility

After you initiate your sexual life with your man, you can use his sexual cycle to your advantage. One man may need sex a number of times every day to feel fulfilled while another will be completely happy indulging once a month or less. The man with a great need for sex will suffer the same irritability after one day of no sex as the other man would suffer after several months. Do not judge a man sexually by his appearance. A man who appears very sexy may have a very low sex drive, while a man who looks calm and quiet may be a temporarily satisfied sexual dynamo.

To determine whether the two of you are sexually compatible, ascertain your man's natural sex cycle and see if you want to meet it. To find the minimum limit of his cycle, just keep saying "Honey, we should wait until tomorrow." There will come a day that he will refuse to postpone sex any longer, or he will become very argumentative over the postponement. The time period that elapses between a mild acceptance of delay and a complaining reaction indicates the outer range of his sexual needs, and you can use the reverse technique to find the maximum limit of his sexual cycle. Simply initiate frequent sexual contact and increase the frequency until he refuses sex. (You may have an exhausted man on your hands until he recovers!)

One woman who wanted to determine her boyfriend's true cycle suggested that they not see each other for ten days, but asked him to call her if he wanted to see her. He had called by the third day and she had her answer.

Try to keep your man on his sexual cycle. Occasionally stretch the cycle a day or two to build up added intensity, or reduce the cycle to diminish the risk that he will wander, particularly if he is going on a trip without you. You will lose your boyfriend, though, if you continuously exhaust him sexually. If your sexual cycle is higher than his, and you press him for sex, he will dismiss you as a nymphomaniac. Similarly, you will lose him if you do not provide him with sufficient sex. If your sexual cycle is lower than your boyfriend's and you deny him sex, he will dismiss you as frigid.

A man judges what is normal based on his own

needs. If it becomes difficult for him to keep you satisfied, he will feel inadequate and you will be passed by. If it becomes difficult for him to achieve his own satisfaction, you will also be passed by.

Praising Sexual Performance

If you spent the day preparing a scrumptious meal for a man and he offered not even the slightest inkling of enjoyment, gratitude, or appreciation, chances are you would not invite him again. Similarly, praise a man's sexual performance when you can and expect him to praise yours.

A man seeks reassurance about his sexual performance, since sex is rarely a passive act for him. Once he has exhausted the excess sexuality of his early youth, he views his time and energy as valuable. The better you make him feel about sex with you, the higher you will rate with him. Saying "Honey, you're terrific" can make the difference in your relationship. If sex has been unsatisfactory over an extended period, you may be wrong for each other. But if it's good, tell him so.

After intercourse, the man will have little energy left. Let him sleep if he wishes. Then, be prepared to revive him with coffee, sweets, and appetizing snacks. When your man achieves sexual satisfaction early in the day, he may be exhausted for hours. If you don't revive him, you may find yourself spending the day with a grouch. If you have sex at night, his body naturally recovers energy in sleep. By morning, his need for you is returning and he will be on par.

Don't Use Sex as a Weapon

Sex, like the hydrogen bomb, is too powerful to be used as a weapon except in the most extreme circumstances. Do not use sex as a weapon. Once you have had sex with a man, do not deny him sex to win an argument or get a gift. Don't even hint of withholding sex to have your way! This is a mistake many women make. Some women believe in giving great samples of sex, then withholding sex until the man commits, the idea being that if the man knows what he is missing, he'll suffer more and want to be back in her bed sooner. But sex is a primary consideration for men and they distrust women who use it as a weapon against them. If you would deny sex to him as his girlfriend, he will think that you will be even meaner to him as his wife. Any threat of selfishly withholding sex will destroy his thoughts of marrying you, and if you are inconsistent in sex, you are in double jeopardy of losing your man.

Let's look at a man's sexual expectation. Sandy has been dating Harry for a while, and they see each other once a week. They had sex together during their past three dates. Is Harry going to expect sex with Sandy on date four? You had better believe it. If Harry is unfulfilled, he will eventually go elsewhere.

If you are ill or are otherwise unable to perform, let your man know the specifics. If you don't tell him what is troubling you, he is likely to think that you are withholding sex. Don't just tell him that "I have a headache" or "I don't feel like it tonight." Be specific. Let him know that you are in trauma over the death of a relative, that you are suffering severe menstrual cramps, that you have an earache, or whatever the problem actually is.

Sexual exclusivity brings with it responsibility for

the other person's sexual satisfaction. In essence, the person who doesn't want sex needs to convince the other person to forgo sexual satisfaction. It's not enough to say "I don't feel like it." If either of you denies sex to the other without a good reason, the other will be frustrated within the relationship, and may begin to look elsewhere.

After Me—Make It Coffee or Tea

A man behaves quite differently when he is satisfied than when he is sexually hungry. After sex, he may not be as considerate. If you are eager to ask a favor from him, or want to press an issue that will require his giving in, ask him before he is sexually exhausted.

Sex and Your Period

Yes, you can have sex with your man during your period. Here is what you need to know:

1. Let the man know you are having a period, particularly if you have reached an age where this will surprise him. Give him a chance to postpone sex. Even today, some men refrain from sex during a woman's period.

2. Most men will have sex with a woman during her period, but many avoid oral sex during that time of the month.

3. Don't let your first encounter with a man happen during your period. Most women are not at their best at that time.

BEDROOM MANNERS

Here are ten tips for improving your bedroom manners and enhancing the sexual aspects of your relationship:

1. Don't destroy romantic illusions. Give him the option of undressing you. He may prefer to undress you slowly since that is more erotic.

2. If you are fertile, use birth control that is pleasant for him. Do not expect him to use a condom, unless disease prevention is your primary concern or his. Condoms may dull his senses too much.

3. Don't expect him to sleep on crumpled or wet sheets. Fix up the bed!

4. Give him his own new toothbrush. There is a limit to intimacy!

5. Never complain about his sexual performance, unless you are willing to end the relationship. Praise him and encourage him when possible.

6. If he has difficulty getting or maintaining an erection, assure him that you care for him and that he will perform beautifully when he is more relaxed.

7. Let him rest or sleep after sex.

8. Do not ridicule the size of his penis or compare him unfavorably to other men.

9. Don't store trinkets or money in your underwear.

10. If he must leave before resting, offer him sweet snacks, which provide bursts of energy.

SEX AND THE STAGNANT RELATIONSHIP

Are you in a relationship that is going nowhere? Is the man enjoying sex with you but seeking nothing further?

A man may seek a long sexual relationship with a woman he does not plan to marry. He does not view himself as investing his time, but he may be wasting yours. Ask yourself whether the relationship has reached a plateau or whether it is progressing. If there is never any reference to a future together, it's best for you to move on.

LIVING TOGETHER

Should you live together before you are married? The answer is unabashedly and unashamedly yes, but there are some limitations on living together, and you should know them before you begin.

The best surprise after marriage is no surprise. Use the living-together portion of the relationship as the final step in the process of selecting your ideal mate.

Benefits From Living Together

Sex is only one benefit from living together; the primary benefits are nonsexual. Use this opportunity to see how you and your potential spouse get along together in close confinement. See how you share household bills and household chores as well as responsibility for decision making.

Most important, use the living-together relationship to discover your future spouse's personal habits. These are some of the questions you should be able to answer about your future spouse before you make the final decision to marry:

1. What are his best times of the day? His worst?

2. What is his favorite time for dinner? For love-making?

3. Does he have difficulty sleeping?

4. Does he snore? How loudly?

5. Does he have a late-night snack in bed? Does he leave crumbs?

6. What time of the day does he shower? Does he enjoy showering with you?

7. Does he hog the bathroom or squeeze the toothpaste in the middle of the tube? Are the hairs in the sink driving you to drink?

8. Is he on the phone at all hours with his friends, family, and colleagues?

9. Does he decide to do exercise or perform religious rituals at times you consider inopportune.

10. Does he treat two-thirds of the bed as his turf? Or seize the blanket for his exclusive use?

These are just a few of the many things you should be learning about the person you live with. You should know him well enough to write a detailed hour-by-hour description of the way he lives.

Occasionally, you may run into someone who opposes living together on moral grounds, but fear is often disguised as morality. A man who is old-fashioned may think poorly of a woman who wants to live with him. If you make an issue of living together, you may lose him, but you may be better off. Before you marry him, reexamine whether such a person can be a suitable mate for you.

Sexual behavior rarely changes significantly after marriage, either in terms of frequency or satisfaction. If you haven't established a pleasurable sex life with your partner before marriage, don't expect a happy sex life afterward.

Premarital sex is important for the woman because she needs to assess the man's performance. He may be able to hide his sexual inadequacies when you are dating, but not when you are living together. If he has been talking a good line but not performing, you can use the living-together relationship to find him out.

Immersion

If you can't live with your prospective spouse, at least make sure to have an immersion period. Be together for one uninterrupted week, twenty-four hours per day. Be in contact with the outside world if you must, but spend as much time alone with him as you can. Two weeks are preferable, but one week should give you a great deal of insight into what your future together would be like. Problems that could develop in your future marriage will probably surface during that week, so that after only one week of immersion, you should know whether you will want him on a permanent basis.

How Long to Live Together

Can living together work against you for marriage? It can, if it starts too soon or continues too long.

As a rule of thumb, do not live with someone until you have known him for six months. Then, live together for at least a month, but not more than a year, if you want to marry him. A relationship peaks and then plateaus. If this happens before marriage, you both will be settled in, and the impetus for marriage will be gone.

When people live together for many years and then marry, these marriages often do not last. These relationships have peaked and plateaued long ago, and may well be on the decline. The couple may try to use a marriage ceremony to save their relationship, but it is usually too late.

Living together also loses many of its benefits if the couple avoids chores and potential conflicts. Be yourself when you live together, and encourage your partner to do so as well. Confront daily life together, head-on.

CHAPTER 10

Tying the Knot

Now we've come to the final step, leading the relationship to marriage. Before you take this step, be sure your man is the man of your choice.

TEACHING HIM TO BE A HUSBAND

Men don't start out as husbands. They must be taught. Here are ten techniques you can use to show him that you are beautiful, intelligent, and his ideal mate, and that you need each other for happiness. Use these skills to make his relationship with you an unbreakable habit.

1. ASSOCIATION. The mind can learn to associate two unrelated events. A Russian scientist by the name of Pavlov rang a bell when he fed his dogs. Later, when he just rang the bell, the dogs salivated because they expected food. You can use this association process in your relationship. Let your man associate a song with a pleasurable moment, a color with a specific effect, an outfit with an event, or a

tone of voice with a mood. If you consistently wear the same perfume or cologne, the man will associate the aroma with you. If he smells this fragrance when you are apart, he will think of you. Similarly, if the two of you have your own song, he will think of you whenever he hears it.

2. INTENSITY. Intense experience teaches quickly. A child who is bitten by a dog may later be fearful of dogs and may even be frightened by a picture of a dog. Any intense event leaves us with an emotional response to the people, places, or objects involved. You can use an intense pleasurable response to work your way into his heart. When he does something pleasing that you would like him to repeat, overreact in some special manner. Jump up and down, hug and kiss him, and cook him his favorite dinner. He is virtually compelled to repeat his pleasing actions.

3. REPETITION. Repetition is the primary source of habits and attitudes and is used extensively by advertisers, teachers, and others. Use this technique by making constant reminders of your beauty and talents. Let your man know that others tell you that you have beautiful hair, or a good mind, or a keen sense of humor. Mention whatever features he responds to favorably. If you are really clever, develop a slogan or motto regarding your relationship, just as clubs and organizations use slogans to unite their members. Repeat the slogan whenever you want to remind him that you are a couple; work your "theme" into activities you share, presents you give him, notes you leave in the morning. ("It's you and me against the world," "We've only just begun," "I've got you, babe," "We're in this together," "Together forever" are a few examples—but the best one will come out of your own experience.)

4. REWARDS. A seal performs for the reward of a fish, a monkey for a banana, a squirrel for a nut, and you and your man perform on the job for paychecks. You can also reward him for his behavior toward you when he does something you like. Give him a superbig hug, smile, or kiss; he will probably repeat his action often enough so that it becomes a habit with him. Do not use sex as a reward, however, just as you should never withhold sex as punishment.

5. PRAISE. Men respond to praise. Every time your man does something you like, give praise. Words are ideal for they can be given anytime, anywhere, and without cost.

6. COMMANDS. A strong voice with a commanding tone gets results. A bellowing "How could you do that?" to something you dislike or "Fantastic!" to something you do like can be effective.

7. SWEET DEMANDS. You can also teach him what it is like to be a husband if you preface your demands with "Honey, you should" or "Please, darling." Saying "Honey, you should cut the grass Saturday," especially if you start a few days before the lawn needs cutting, will get the grass cut on Saturday.

8. EXHAUSTION. We are especially susceptible to suggestions when we are exhausted. If you tell your man at six P.M. that you are lovely, perhaps by repeating a compliment you received from someone else, he may have the mental energy to fight off this thought. At three A.M., his resistance is lower and he may not be able to reject your claim to loveliness. Use this time to implant the idea of your importance to him and the thought that you would

be a perfect wife. This is the time to deliver your sales pitch.

9. Moods. A man can learn love and happiness with you. Your moods affect his behavior. If you appear happy whenever you are with your man, he will feel welcome and wanted by you at all times. Knowing he brings you joy will keep him by your side.

10. Example. One of the best ways you can teach a man to be a good husband is for you to be a good wife. You need to start this process before you are married.

CREATING INTERDEPENDENCE

The key to mutual love is interdependence. Your relationship will thrive only if the man meets your needs and you meet his. Need is one of the most important facets of love. People rarely love someone unless they also need them.

Do not marry a man who does not meet your needs. Prepare your own list, using this list of seven physical and seven emotional needs as a starting point, and decide if he is right for you.

Your Physical Needs

1. How much sex do you need to feel comfortable and relaxed? Is this level of sexual activity compatible with his needs and capacities?

2. How much care do you require to keep yourself, your clothing, and your nest in order? Do you have

sufficient energy to carry out your usual daily tasks, or will you be counting on his energy to help you? How much care does he need?

3. What foods will you cheerfully eat? Could you deal with his eating patterns, or would you resent not having your usual fare?

4. How much sleep do you require to feel your best? Will your need for sleep or his be a problem? Could you sleep with the light or the television on, or must there be total quiet and darkness? Does his pattern match yours?

5. What are your needs for rest and physical exercise? Does it match his pattern?

6. What home-entertainment activities do you enjoy? Do your preferences irrate him? Do his activities annoy you?

7. How often do you like to socialize? Do his plans conflict with yours?

Your Emotional Needs

1. Are you both angered by the same things and to the same extent? Will you feed each other's angers, or help each other cope?

2. How well-matched is your sense of humor to his? Can it help you over the rough times? Will you resent his capacity to laugh? Will he resent your joviality?

3. How much ego-bruising do each of you get on the job? How much ego-stroking will you need from each other?

4. What are the things that make you feel guilty? Will he understand your guilt feelings?

5. Will you be jealous of his desire to spend time with old friends or friends from work?

6. How will you react if his job takes priority over other plans?

7. In what areas do you need to feel superior to him or to other individuals in his life? When do you need him to be superior?

Meeting His Needs

You must meet his needs, just as he must meet yours, if the marriage is to flourish. Do you meet his needs? Every man has four primary kinds of needs: physical, intellectual, emotional, and goal-oriented.

First, fulfill the man's physical needs. Help provide comforts. Make sure that he has proper rest and healthful activities. Provide stimulation for all five of his senses. Most definitely, in time, include sex.

Second, satisfy the man's intellectual needs. A man needs to be with a similarly intelligent mate. Otherwise, he will feel alone. You must match his intellectual expectations. If you do not know as much about something as he does, ask him to teach you. Do the same for him.

Third, fulfill the man's emotional needs. If his emotions are not stimulated with praise and criticism, he can become frustrated or bored, and if he is bored, you are likely to lose him.

Fourth, help the man achieve those goals that he believes he must reach at any cost. If you hinder rather than help him, he will pass you by for marriage.

Creating More Needs

Discover the desires your man has that do not reach the level of being needs. Then, decide which of these desires you can fulfill. Once you have identified these desires, you may be able to convert some of them into needs. If so, you may be able to increase his dependency on you.

Create needs that you can fulfill. You may be in the position, for instance, of convincing him that his wardrobe needs updating or that his play needs a new musical score. If you are a good shopper, he will ask you to select his new clothes; if you are a musician, he'll ask you to write the musical score for his play. Your likelihood of success is greater if his needs are unique and you are uniquely qualified to fulfill them.

To uncover and discover other needs, probe into his motivations for independence, especially as a youngster, and his long-term goals. Remember, you can elicit this information most effectively if you ask first about the past, then the future, and finally the present.

A woman who truly wants a man will encourage him to rely on her to enhance his life, and the man will learn to do this in return. Of course, if the dependency is too great in either direction, you may be unsuitable as mates.

Be Indispensable

One of the most important techniques for leading a man into marriage is to become indispensable to him. Being indispensable does not mean being subservient. Avoid menial tasks unless these tasks are essential or you genuinely enjoy doing them.

Here are ten ways in which you can become indispensable:

1. Edit his reports.

2. Cook his favorite meal.

3. Select clothing for him.

4. Balance his checkbook.

5. Help him keep up with political ideas.

6. Get to know his family, friends, and business contacts.

7. Be available in emergencies.

8. Participate in his hobbies—be a fourth for bridge or tennis even if you don't particularly like the game.

9. Make constructive criticisms, but only in private.

10. Tell the world how wonderful he is—be his P.R. person.

There are very significant differences between individuals. An act that one person would consider indispensable, someone else would consider annoying or worse. Before you attempt to make yourself indispensable to a particular man, discover his particular needs when you interview him. Remember, "desires" are different from needs, so focus first upon his "needs" when you can. Then, look to his desires and yours.

His Need to Be Needed

If your man is like most men, he wants to be needed. In fact, he *needs* to be needed. He may even stay with a woman he doesn't truly want because she needs him. If a woman does not show need for a man, he may avoid a relationship, even if he wants her. If you want him, show your need for him.

What is this "need to be needed"? Is it chivalry, male chauvinism, or some entirely different phenomenon? In fact, it is the reverse of chivalry or even male chauvinism. This need relates directly to male insecurities and the rejection that boys suffered during adolescence at the hands of girls.

Men fear rejection by women, and want to minimize their risk of rejection. A man seeks a woman who needs him because this woman is less likely to reject him. If you ask a typical man, "Why do you want to marry a woman who needs you?" he will respond, "If she doesn't need me, she might leave me."

An insecure man may offer a woman furs, jewelry, or other worldly goods in his attempt to obtain her loyalty. The more insecure the man, the more he feels the need to buy the woman's attention and affection with possessions. His unconscious strategy is to induce the woman to need him and become dependent on him. Yet he cannot buy genuine love.

Interdependence

Before you started your relationship, each of you lived totally independent of the other. Now both of you should be happier because of your mutual companionship. The more the two of you share your talents and strengths, the stronger the relationship becomes. Interdependence is the culmination of your personal development. Consider these three steps to personal maturity:

1. Dependence

2. Independence

3. Interdependence

From your earliest beginnings, you were dependent on others, especially your parents. Most of you eventually strove for, and attained, your independence. You proved to the world, and to yourself, that you could survive and thrive on your own. Now you can use the inner strength that you developed from achieving independence while regaining the earlier joys of dependency. Interdependence is your key to self-fulfillment.

The successful woman generally prides herself on her independence. She is likely to believe that she can satisfy most, if not all, of her needs. She often provides her own food, shelter, and entertainment. In fact, if she wants children, she may even have considered, but most likely rejected, single motherhood. If she wants total independence from men, surely that has cost her marriage.

Don't be afraid of saying to a man, "I need you to do this for me!" If it is not an overwhelming burden to him, he will respond to your request, but don't exploit him. He will want you to be appreciative of his efforts and benefit from his talents. So balance what he does for you by doing "your thing" for him.

The man needs some assurance that he is irreplaceable in your life, so that it is safe for him to love you. He knows you will not readily pull away from commitment if you need him. The man also enjoys the ego recognition that comes from feeling so needed. But do not become a burden. That is *not* what he wants.

You achieve interdependence when two things happen: You begin to depend on him for the things he does best and will do willingly, and he begins to depend on you for things you do best and will do willingly. Sit down with your future mate and discuss how you enrich each other's lives. Think about the areas in which you and he complement each other. Does he fulfill enough of your needs to make you a happier person as a result? Do you fulfill his needs to the point that he is delighted with you? Balance the added effort it takes to have a mate with the added comforts that having a mate provides. Your life and his should be happier as a result of your togetherness.

Marriage is a lot like getting into a lifeboat with your mate. You should be sure that you will row in the same direction, that neither of you will drop anchor or row in the opposite direction. The more you help him in achieving his goals, and the more he helps you in achieving yours, the greater the probability is that you will have a successful marriage.

MARRIAGE ATTITUDES

A man expects certain attitudes from his wife. You need to display these attitudes to him if you are serious about marriage.

Work

Most men have to work for a living. In their work, they deal with an outside world that often is exhausting and frustrating. A man expects to work to support himself and may expect the same from his wife. Show your willingness to help him or to work for a living. Do not be an anchor around his neck or a prima donna who won't pitch in.

Demonstrate to the man that you are an asset, not a liability, that you also have a work ethic, and that you will help in your mutual survival.

Parents

Our parents cared for us when we were youngsters, and the time may come when we may have to care for them when they reach old age. This is the cycle of life, whether we like it or not. The man may have responsibilities to either or both of his parents and may worry that you will resent the time and expense he has to spend on his folks.

It is the duty of one spouse to help the other provide care for elderly parents. It may not be pleasant to sit with your man through the aging and death of his parents, but it is part of your marital duties. Indicate by your own behavior and attitudes toward your own elderly relatives that you will willingly take on this responsibility if it becomes necessary, and expect him to do the same for you.

His Children

The man you want may have children. You have several emotional hurdles to overcome with his children, but his children can become a great source of joy for you.

The female, by nature, usually has strong love instincts for her child, whether or not she really cares for the child's father. The male, on the other hand, initially loves the child to the same degree that he loves the child's mother.

Do not be too surprised if your man does not have strong paternal instincts. Some men do, others do not. However, this does not mean that you can be indifferent to his children. You must treat them in a very loving manner, as if you were their mother. Remember, if you marry the man, you are expected to be a loving parent to his children and a loving grandparent to his grandchildren.

One of the greatest errors a woman can make is to show hostility to a man's children from a previous marriage. The children are the innocent victims of a love relationship that went sour. Do not criticize their mother in their presence. Any unkind remarks or attitudes toward the natural mother will build resentment toward you from the children.

Every child wishes that his natural parents would get together again. As kind and as thoughtful as you are to his children, they would still displace you if it meant that their mom and dad had a chance at reconciliation. They may even say so loudly. Don't be offended! Bide your time, for when you marry and the children see that you do not plan to overrun their father or push them out of his life, they will become supportive and respectful of you.

Children require tender love and care as well as expense, patience, and extraordinary energy and time. When you are dealing with his or your children from a previous marriage, the man needs to know that you are a good parent. Determine what he expects a good mother to do and to be. Do not act indifferent, mean, or lacking in joy when you deal with his children or yours; you'll be passed by for marriage if children are important to him, especially if he is looking to start a family. Furthermore, a man will assume that if you are mean to children, you will also be mean to him.

Pets

You may find it hard to believe, but many men identify with pets. If you are cruel to your pet or his, the man will fear that you are capable of the same cruelty toward him. Turn this concept to your advantage by fussing over any pet, especially his. Even if the man scowls when you fuss with his pet, he will appreciate your considerate behavior and respond as if the kindness were directed at him.

FEATHERING THE FUTURE NEST

You want your future mate to invest time, energy, and emotions in your future. Create fond memories and build your personal history together. Encourage projects that will carry over into the marriage. Build things together that will carry over to a mutual nest, such as a bookcase or other piece of furniture.

Suppose you have a dog and you know he likes dogs. Ask him to wash Rover for you. The first time, he is doing you a favor. The second time, he is doing Rover a favor. The third time, it's "his dog." Let him invest those emotions.

Share the responsibilities of daily life. The more time and energy he invests in you, the more likely he is to continue. If you can balance a checkbook better than he can, do his. If he is a better shopper than you are, let him do the shopping. The more familiar he is with the lifestyle and surroundings he will have when you marry, the easier the transition will be.

YOUR "SALES PITCH"

The woman who does not claim superiority about herself loses out. The man expects a "sales pitch" and may think the woman lacks interest in him if he doesn't hear one.

Now is the time to show him your superiorities. A man is likely to diminish your claims, so build up your assertions to compensate. This way you should come out even in his judgment of you.

Some sales managers tell their salespeople to "throw enough mud against the wall and some of it will stick." Many politicians use the same technique. Enhance yourself and your desirability by throwing enough positive ideas about yourself at him that many will stick.

You can convince the man of your choice to marry you if you make the right sales pitch at the right time. Both timing and substance are crucial. Tell him the many reasons why he should marry you. Let him know that your goals are compatible with his and that you can foresee a happy future together.

Establishing Your Uniqueness

Just as it is important for you to recognize your man's uniqueness, it is important for him to recognize yours. You may have one or more of these superior features:

Good dancer	Liveliness
Beautiful eyes	Good voice
Good listener	Funster
Neat housekeeper	Musical ability
Good sense of humor	Athletic ability
Interesting conversationalist	Intelligence
Good cook	Good mother
Kindness	Ambition
Career success	Professional recognition
Firm breasts	Shapely legs

Ascertain your superior qualities, then determine which of these qualities will appeal to the man and accentuate them. This is one of the most important steps in "selling" yourself to him. When you interviewed him for the job of husband, you determined which qualities he was seeking. Now let him know that you have the special qualities he desires.

Getting Him to Think About the Future

Some men take life or work so seriously that they do not devote adequate attention to their women. They do not think about marriage. However, these men can be led toward marriage if you can change their focus.

If your boyfriend works too hard or takes life more seriously than he should, take him to a cemetery to sober him into reality. Your best bet is to visit the grave of one of his departed relatives. If that isn't feasible, visit an old historic graveyard or a national cemetery, where visitors are common. You want him to realize that he will not live forever and that he should be thinking about his personal future, including marriage to you. As he reads headstones, he will reflect on his own mortality.

If you cannot drag your man to a cemetery, use other techniques to remind him of his fleeting existence on the face of the earth. Ask him what he'd like his tombstone to say. Ask if he would prefer cremation. Subtly remind him that his next heartbeat may be his last. Start with a comment such as "Isn't it amazing that we go about our lives so casually?" Ask him how much fun has he really experienced so far, and ask him what he'd like to do with the rest of his life.

RAISING THE TOPIC OF MARRIAGE

You want the idea of marriage to occur to your man and for him to bring it up. However, since you can't leave anything to chance, the next best option is for the idea of marriage to be brought up by others. Let the world suggest marriage.

When marriage talk is timely and he has not mentioned a wedding, go to places where the world will treat the two of you as married. Look at big-ticket items that he will enjoy seeing and that are usually bought by married couples, such as motor homes, condominiums, boats, cars, or large-screen television sets. The salesperson, trying to sell goods, will paint a very rosy picture of you and your husband living at Heavenly Ranch Estates, or will point out how much your children will enjoy the new TV. Don't bother to correct the salesperson. Instead, wink or look amused at your man. Later you can refer to the fact you two are starting to "look married."

Try to become involved with his family occasions so that you can favorably impress his parents. Meet his nieces and nephews. Someone in his family is likely to say

"I wonder what your children would look like." His family will start him thinking.

Describe an optimistic future for him with you in it. Make such statements as "If you and I combined our efforts and talents, there isn't anything we couldn't accomplish." Talk about the safari you are planning together next year, or the vacation home you both could own in three years. If he wants a beautiful home, pick up a magazine with pictures of desirable houses to fire his imagination. Do the same for other interests he has.

Behave as if you already are his wife. Let him depend on you as he would depend on a wife, and act as his partner in fighting off the cruel world. Determine his image of the perfect mate and take on the part! If he is in business and must entertain, learn to be a good hostess and help him. Fuss at his dress, tell him his hair needs to be trimmed, comment on his manners, and carry on as you would with a husband.

THE PROPOSAL

Chances are that every married woman you know, especially your mother, told you a tale about how her husband got down on bended knee and romantically asked for her hand in marriage. The truth would be more interesting, but rarely will a woman admit to the wiles she used to get her man, and even more rarely will she admit that she orchestrated the proposal.

Marriage is not caused by spontaneous combustion. A couple usually reaches a point where they act as though they were married and live as though they were married, but something else must occur for them to actually *decide* to marry. Usually, after being together for six months to a year, it's time to move into marriage. If your partner is spending all of his free time with you, the relationship is sexually exclusive, you are openly communicative, and you are living as if you were married, then it's time for a proposal.

If the proposal is left to you, here's how to handle it. Tell your partner, "Honey, I just enjoy life so much when we're together, that if you don't propose to me within the next few months, I'll propose to you." The best time of the year to get a commitment from a man is between Thanksgiving and New Year's because these holidays center around family life. The wedding may take place in the summer, but the commitment is made in November or December. When your man asks you what you want for Christmas, be sure to say "you." Do not say "a ring." "A ring" sounds too materialistic to a man who is about to give himself to you.

Avoid blatant ultimatums, but you don't need to be subtle either. One woman told her live-in partner, "The next trip we take together will be our honeymoon," and it was. I told my husband in October that he could choose the wedding date as long as it was within that calendar year. We married December 30th.

YOUR ENGAGEMENT

Relationships grow and develop into marriage, passing through a number of stages, including the engagement. Your engagement is the transition period between single life and marriage. The engagement begins with the decision to marry, the announcement, and perhaps a ring, and includes celebrations, wedding plans, and serious discussions about your future life together.

It takes effort to be engaged, just as it took effort to become engaged. This transition to marriage is often difficult, and many engagements are broken because the woman took the man for granted during the engagement.

The Ring

You do not need a ring to be engaged, but engagement rings are commonplace. However, be cautious when selecting a ring. Many women are looking forward to large diamonds to show off to their friends, but your man may consider requests for diamonds as displays of greed. Many engagements have ended here. If he does buy you a diamond, put his mind at ease by telling him that the ring is his, and he can have it back at any time. Or show your man that you are considerate of his finances by suggesting cubic zirconium rather than diamond. Tell him that you will wear the ring proudly, regardless of its price.

If he does bring you a large diamond, he may do so to show off his status and success, or to intimidate other men and make you less approachable. Do not let the ring inflate your ego. Remember, another woman could wear the diamond. The ring neither enhances nor detracts from your true uniqueness.

If the ring was selected by the man, do not have the stone appraised and brag to your friends about how much it's worth. Your friends may discuss your actions publicly, and your man may find out about the appraisal. This is a common error and a real insult to the man. He views himself as the prize he is awarding you, and if you place too much emphasis on the ring, he will feel you are diminishing *his* importance.

Celebrations

The engagement is an occasion for celebration, but it is also the opportunity to become accustomed to each other. Do not let festivities obscure the reality of day-to-day living. Your man, not your friends, should be first in your life. Do not let your friends overshadow his importance. If he is not first in your life, do not marry him.

Duration

The engagement has no minimum or maximum duration. You and your future husband have much to accomplish during this period before marriage, so make sure the engagement period is long enough. However, there is no advantage to an overly long engagement except in unusual situations. In general, a three-month period for the engagement is preferable, but this rule of thumb is merely the starting point for your own schedule. If you are young, in school, separated by a long distance, or in financial distress, the engagement period should probably be longer.

Your boyfriend may be shy and may balk at the social frills involved in a wedding. To test your love for him, he may suggest that you elope. If he does, tell him that you will! You might mention that your deposit on the hall may be lost and that friends and family will be disappointed, but do not refuse to elope. Do not marry someone with whom you would not elope.

Sex and Exclusivity

If everything has been moving in the right direction, you've been having sexual relations for some time before becoming engaged. Even among people who oppose sex before marriage, sex during engagement is widely accepted. Moreover, sexual relations are important at this stage as you must determine if you and he can adjust to each other's needs.

Begin living together while you are engaged if you are not already doing so. Before you are married, you should be sure that you and your man have compatible lifestyles. Try to spend as much time together as possible. If your relationship is not already sexually exclusive, it should become so once you are engaged.

The Dastardly Act

The man may be angry with himself for falling in love. He may be absolutely enthralled with you, but he may be thinking wistfully of the millions of women he has not yet encountered and must now permanently forgo. In fact, he may be so angry that he may do something mean to you on the brink of marriage. He may, perhaps subconsciously, want to test you to be sure that you really love him. If you are prepared for such a "dastardly act" you can ride out the storm. He soon will revert to his sweet, lovable self. Women who do not understand men will misread the dastardly act and end the relationship.

These are three of the most extreme dastardly acts I have ever seen in the course of developing a marriage relationship:

1. Slashing the tires of her car

2. Moving to Europe

3. Showing up at his wedding with a date (not his bride)

Even my own husband committed a dastardly act. He refused to wear a tie to our wedding. Whether the act is cruel or just symbolic, realize that it is simply the man's last gesture of resistance before marriage. Don't let yourself react negatively; you're on the right track!

What to Know and Admit Before Marriage

This is a checklist of crucial information that prospective mates should know about each other before making a marriage commitment, the ten things you *must* know about the person you marry. Surprisingly, many people who marry do not even know this much about each other.

1. Age

2. Obligations to support or care for others, such as former spouses, children, or parents

3. Marital status and prior relationships

4. Children (natural and adopted)

5. Religious beliefs ·

6. Sexual expectations

7. Financial situation, including assets, liabilities, and income

8. Attitude toward each other's ethnic background

9. Values placed upon money, fidelity, family loyalty

10. "Skeletons in the closet" that may later cause public embarrassment

This information is not always readily ascertainable. Each prospective spouse, however, has the right to know the true situation of the other person, to determine the probability of a successful marriage and the possible areas of major conflicts.

This information should not be discussed at the outset of dating, but should be discussed long before engagement. You and your partner will try to cooperate to resolve potential conflicts, but conflicts on this list sometimes cannot be resolved.

It is not advisable to discuss all potential conflicts at the same time. These revelations can be emotionally negative. Discuss this information over a period of at least a few months. In this manner, you both will have the time you need to get used to each other's situations.

If you have listened carefully to your man's stories and you have asked the right questions, and you have not criticized, condemned, or ridiculed his responses, you will probably already have insight into his responses to the items on this list.

YOUR WEDDING

Your wedding plans should solidify your relationship and enable you to start your marriage on a strong foundation. All too often, however, an impending wedding weakens rather than strengthens the relationship. In fact, your wedding is the last opportunity before marriage to frighten the man into remaining a bachelor.

A woman may mishandle her wedding if she does not keep the interests of her man clearly in mind. These mistakes are made most commonly by young women who have never been married before. A woman may have fantasized about her wedding from the time she was a young girl. She pictures the details of the ceremony, from her wedding dress to her bridal bouquet. She knows who she wants to invite, how she wants the invitations to read, and which guests she wants to sit together. She views the wedding day as her day, with little if any thought of the groom and his desires. This attitude will strike the man as immature and selfish.

The cost of the wedding was traditionally borne by the bride's family and the wedding plans were traditionally made by the bride. Today, however, many men have their own idea about the wedding, and these ideas must also be considered in making wedding plans. At the very least, consult with the man about major aspects of the wedding ceremony.

Some women believe that their future husband should not see them in their wedding dress, or should not see them on their wedding day before the ceremony. These traditions are destructive, because it makes the man feel left out and destroys some of the necessary closeness between the man and woman.

A big wedding poses an especially great danger to the relationship. Often, the bride devotes so much time and energy to the wedding plans that she neglects her intended husband. Yet it is at this time that the man most needs her attention and reassurances of her love.

Your wedding is the beginning of your married life, not just the end of your single life. Make it enjoyable for your husband too. The woman should remember that the wedding day is not her day. It's *their* day!

Family Interference

You may be facing family interference when you are planning to marry. If so, develop a response.

If your parents condemn your future husband because of their personal prejudices, don't let them dissuade you. Don't drop him just because they said so. If your mother is discouraging you, she may be doing so because she is lonely. Keep conditioning her to your man. Even if you are not initially successful, in time she will probably accept him as your husband.

Your children, or your future husband's children, may also have objections, but don't let them interfere with your marriage plans. Tell them that while you're sorry to hear that they feel this way, you hope that they will come to see that you truly want and need this relationship for your own happiness, and that you hope your happiness is important to them. Children from his previous marriage may be your greatest source of Mother's Day greetings once they learn you are not an ogre who will devour their father.

The Marriage Contract

A marriage contract is an agreement between the future husband and the future wife that identifies their rights, responsibilities, and property ownership; this contract should also settle all questions of financial responsibility between the spouses. Before you get married, a lawyer should help you draw up a marriage contract. Your man will need a lawyer, too.

A decade ago, marriage contracts were relatively uncommon except when one of the individuals was wealthy or where there were children from a prior marriage. Marriage contracts are becoming more popular today, even when the bride and groom are young and neither has been married previously. The major reason for the upswing in their popularity is the changing role of women in American society.

For most of us, marriage is the most important legal relationship we will ever enter into, even more important than buying a house or forming a business of our own. You may well find it to your advantage to protect yourself and your future husband through a marriage contract.

Your future husband may be aware of his need for a marriage contract, especially if he is wealthy or is success-ful in his business or profession. Even if you are not seeking a marriage contract, he may expect you to sign such an agreement, so you had better be prepared to discuss your expectations.

Conclusion

Now that you have come to the end of this book, you are ready to begin your search for the man of your choice. If you follow our advice, marriage will be well within your grasp. Prepare yourself for the work that is ahead of you, because some of the techniques will take practice and patience. Just remember to keep trying and testing what you have learned, and your endurance will pay off.

Let me know your thoughts and comments, and your experiences in using the book. I can't respond to every letter, but I will try.

From time to time, I run workshops on getting married and staying married. If you are interested in attending, please let me know.

You now have the knowledge to attract the men you want. It's time to turn your dreams into action. Go out there and get the man of your choice!

And, of course, do send me a wedding announcement!

Margaret Kent
Suite 300
104 Crandon Boulevard
Key Biscayne, FL 33149

ABOUT THE AUTHOR

Margaret Kent is an attorney in Key Biscayne, Florida. Her law practice includes matrimonial matters, export incentives, and international taxation. She is a member of the Florida Bar and the International Fiscal Association. She received her B.A. from Barry University in Miami, Florida; M.A. from Instituto Technológico de Estudios Superiores de Monterrey in Monterrey, Mexico; and J.D. from the University of Miami Law School.